THE HOLLOW EARTH ENIGMA

The Hollow Earth Enigma

Alec Maclellan

SOUVENIR PRESS

Copyright © 1999 by Seventh Zenith Ltd.

The right of Alec Maclellan to be identified as author
of this work has been asserted by him in accordance with
the Copyright, Designs and Patents Act 1988.

First published 1999 by
Souvenir Press Ltd,
43 Great Russell Street, London WC1B 3PA

ISBN 0 285 63498 4

Typeset by Rowland Phototypesetting Ltd,
Bury St Edmunds, Suffolk

Printed in Great Britain by
The Guernsey Press Co. Ltd., Guernsey, Channel Islands

CONTENTS

This coincidence between scientific arrogance and a new social trend illustrates an important fact in our society: while science consistently refuses to consider phenomena that lie outside the safe regions of its current understanding, the public is eagerly reaching for explanations that fit its experience.

Jacques Vallee
Dimensions (1988)

PROLOGUE

There is an ancient South American legend which relates that around two thousand years ago four brothers and four sisters emerged from a huge cavern that ran into the centre of the earth. The eldest of the men climbed to the top of a mountain in what is now Peru and, taking up four stones, threw them to the four points of the compass. With this act he took possession of the land that lay within his stones' throw and all those who lived there. He also laid the foundations of Cuzco which, in time, would become the capital of the mighty Inca Empire.

According to local tradition, these eight men and women came from a subterranean world and gave to the people the skills in engineering, agriculture, arts and crafts, and the ability to organise their economy and social welfare, which made the Inca dynasty a marvel of pre-Columbian America until it was destroyed by the Spanish invaders. The mysterious benefactors also left a message carved on a stone tablet which has special significance for us in the dawn of the new millennium. It translates:

> *When two thousand years have passed,*
> *Beneath the frozen waters*
> *A new world will be discovered.*

Scholars who have studied the couplet suggest that the reference to 'frozen waters' most probably means the South

Pole; and that the 'new world' recalls a very old belief that an entrance to the fabled Hollow Earth lies there. If true, the prophecy holds out the prospect—at last—of an answer to one of the great enigmas of history and, especially, of the world which mankind inhabits.

One

THE SUBSURFACE WORLD

The Hollow Earth theory was one of the first controversial scientific topics to interest Charles Fort, the American whose books about inexplicable events and phenomena led to the creation of the Fortean Society and, indirectly, hugely successful movies such as *Close Encounters of the Third Kind* and the TV series *The X-Files*. This indefatigable journalist, who spent his life collecting weird and bizarre stories for which science had no ready explanation, was dismissed in some quarters as a crank who championed the most absurd theories; to others, like the English author Eric Frank Russell, he was 'the only real genius sf ever had'.

Fort, who was born in 1874 and died in 1932, dedicated himself to trying to convince people that the world on which we live is a much stranger place than we realise. Although he had no scientific training and culled much of his material from books, newspapers and journals, he believed that humans should be made aware of the undeniably improbable beliefs about the world they inhabited. A quick-witted but often cussed man, he regularly attacked the scientific establishment for dogmatically dismissing unconventional opinions, and ran foul of the establishment for what some saw as alarmist theories that we might all be the 'property' of omniscient aliens. At the age of 43 Fort was suddenly freed from the need to work when he came into a legacy, and thereafter threw himself wholeheartedly into his investigations. The result was a series of ground-breaking works, including *The Book of the Damned* (1919), *New Lands* (1923) and *Wild Talents* (1932), which have subsequently assured his reputation.

It was early on in his research into strange science that Fort first came across references to the Hollow Earth enigma. This immediately excited his interest as a subject worthy of study, and he began planning a work entitled *Y* to investigate the story. Although, sadly, he never completely finished or published the manuscript, in it he started piecing together the main threads of the legend which he discovered had been recorded since Biblical times and even earlier. The facts as he learned them were that the interior of our planet is actually hollow and may have been inhabited since time immemorial. Some accounts he came across suggested that these subterranean people could be the survivors of the lost continents of Atlantis or Mu, who had fled to the underground world when their lands were inundated.

Like others drawn to the remarkable story, Fort learned that investigators had reached the conclusion that the Earth was doughnut-shaped, rather like the Van Allen belts surrounding the planet, and there were a number of theories as to *why* it was not solid, as science claimed, but hollow with a central sun and its own hospitable atmosphere and climate. At the North and South Poles there were believed to be giant 'holes' leading to this world, holes anywhere between 800 to 1,400 miles in diameter at their widest points, curving through a crust of about 900 miles with a gap of about 300 miles at the narrowest point. Through these a sea or air explorer might gain entry. Inside lay a subterranean 'paradise' of oceans and landmasses, as well as rich and fertile countryside able to sustain plant, animal and human life—almost an inverted mirror-image of our own world.

By contrast, the scientific textbooks which Fort consulted told him that the Earth was a solid, oblate spheroid with an equatorial diameter of 7,926 miles and its polar dimension of 7,900 miles. It was thought to consist of an inner core extending to about 800 miles from the centre (possibly consisting of solid iron and nickel), an outer core about 1,400 miles thick (possibly of molten iron and nickel) and a mantle of solid rock about 1,800 miles thick, separated from the outer crust and varying in thickness from three to five miles. The area of land surface of the Earth amounted to 57 million square miles with over 139 million square miles of sea floor. The planet was estimated to weigh six sextillion tons.

The more he read, the more Fort became convinced—as other Hollow Earth researchers have been before and since—that there still had to be an immense region underground that was completely unknown. He challenged 'the conceit and competence of scientists', agreeing with another suggestion that if the Earth was a solid sphere it would surely weigh much more than six sextillion tons. It seemed likely that the core region which science could not fully explain might well have a radius of as much as 2,200 miles—more than enough to accommodate, say, the Moon, which had a diameter of 2,160 miles. So *what* could possibly exist there?

Charles Fort noted all the legends and theories he could find in his manuscript, retelling them in the same highly individualistic style that became his hallmark: a mixture of impressive amounts of data with the occasional direct statement. Although he was always prepared to admit that some of the material he utilised might be dubious, scientifically-speaking, Fort never deviated from his conviction that there was a kind of unity in all things—even, apparently, the most unrelated facts. It might seem crazy to some people to learn that the world was, after all, hollow, but there was still a lot of evidence to support the concept. And if this *was* the case, it provided an explanation for so many of the phenomena he had gathered.

The books by Charles Fort which led to the inauguration of the Fortean Society to continue his work, and later a monthly magazine, *Fortean Times*, have also encouraged subsequent generations of writers to approach all manner of unlikely concepts in an unprejudiced way. People like Graham Hancock, recently described by the *Sunday Times* as 'the Indiana Jones of alternative archaelogy', whose best-selling books, including *Fingerprints of the Gods* (1995) which has sold almost four million copies, and the TV series *Quest for the Lost Civilisation* (1998), have made him into a household name.

In particular, Hancock has proposed the theory that an unknown and highly advanced civilisation which was destroyed in a global cataclysm at the end of the last ice age, around 10,500 BC, may have been responsible for the origins of cultures as far apart as Egypt, Peru, Mexico and Cambodia. The former East African correspondent has certainly brought to light many remarkable facts about ancient wonders such as the megaliths of Britain and France and the great edifices of South America, as well as discovering near the Japanese island of Yonaguni an extraordinary submerged pyramid structure which is believed to have been *above* sea level over 10,000 years ago. Yet remarkable as these discoveries and his conclusions are, I wonder why he has missed—or overlooked—the possibility that the cultural influence of which he speaks might well have been that of people who fled to the Hollow Earth—or, indeed, originated there?

Hancock's books are very much in the same tradition as those of the 'founding fathers' of the latest phase of interest in alternative science, the Swiss writer Erich von Däniken and the American Charles Berlitz. Berlitz became famous with his international best-seller about unexplained disappearances, *The Bermuda Triangle* (1975), and has recently touched on the subject of the Hollow Earth in his *World of Strange Phenomena* (1990): 'Belief in a hollow earth surfaces in many cultures around the world and adherents of the theory point out that many things in nature—bones, pits, fruits and animals, for example—are structured around an inner cavity. Therefore it's logical to assume that the earth is as well.'

Erich von Däniken also arrived on the scene with a world-wide best-seller, *Chariots of the Gods?* (1969), in which he set out to prove that the Earth had been visited by space travellers both before and after the dawn of recorded history. Recently, however, he has shifted his study from the heavens to the Earth itself and believes the answer to what lies in the subsurface world may actually be found by a more accessible route than through the polar apertures.

In an interview in *Encounters* magazine in April 1998, he suggested that there may be an entrance to the subterranean world via the Great Pyramids of Giza in Egypt.

'There are many secrets still be to uncovered in the pyramids,' he said. 'For example, there is an unexplored tunnel shaft which my friend Rudolf Gatenbrink and I investigated in 1993 with the aid of a specially developed, 37cm-long robot camera. It revealed a shaft no human eyes have seen for at least 4,500 years, at the end of which is an ancient doorway. With the use of a laser, Gatenbrink was able to show that this leads to further unexplored space. Could this be the entrance to the subterranean world which has been talked about for thousands of years?'

Von Däniken believes the question will only be answered when the ancient doorway is opened. At the time of writing this seems an unlikely possibility, due to the scepticism of both the Egyptian authorities and a number of leading Egyptologists who do not share his attitude—or that of Charles Fort or Charles Berlitz or any of their ilk for that matter—towards unconventional science, insisting that there is *nothing* there. What all these writers *have* done, however, is help to promote interest in the mystery of the Hollow Earth. Thus prepared, I hope the reader is ready to embark on a quest for knowledge that takes us back to the very birth of our planet.

*　　*　　*

Almost five billion years ago the Earth was just an enormous ball of hot, whirling gases, slowly cooling. According to the laws of physics, cooling gases condense, thereby allowing the 'ball' which would become our planet to coalesce as the heat evaporated. This process, physicists believe, continued in a spiralling whorl so that the self-centred force of gravity gradually reduced the gases until, approximately 2,800 million years ago, they finally became a solid sphere.

Such is the 'solid Earth' concept, and indeed the study of core samples from deep drilling does seem to substantiate this, *although these drillings have only penetrated to limited depths*. Tests have also shown that the temperatures within the Earth increase the deeper the drilling goes, *although again this is true only to the depths that have so far been tapped*. Therefore, traditional science argues, it seems safe to assume that our world is solid from surface to core. But *is* it?

Although this theory is generally accepted for the celestial evolution of huge bodies like stars, it is arguably *not* the last word in the creation of typical planets such as the Earth. Indeed, a quick investigation of centrifugal force throws up an entirely different possibility. Gravity, we know, attempts to draw all material towards the centre, while centrifugal force does the opposite. With this in mind, American Hollow Earth researcher Cate Malone has taken an everyday example to explain what she believes occurred in the creation of our world. Writing in *Exposure* magazine, Volume 3, Number 2, she says:

> Science accepts the fact that the Earth spins on its axis. Centrifugal force makes the Earth bulge slightly at the equator and flatten at the poles. To visualise what the firmation of a planet could look like, think of a washing machine on a spin cycle. The clothing (gases, liquids and particles) are thrown outwards against the sides of the machine (gravity). The centre portion remains clear. The hollow centre is firmed. Just as the Earth has never stopped spinning, so this washing machine never gets out of spin cycle. If the machine continues to spin, will the water and clothes start clumping together in the middle or will they endlessly spin around the hollow centre?

It was this law of motion—centrifugal force—trying to thrust all the material outward from the developing Earth's axis of rotation that ultimately created a balance between the two vast natural forces, Malone explains. And the compromise between them resulted in a hollow rotating sphere approximately 8,000 miles in diameter. There is even more conclusive evidence for this, according to Mark Harp in his article 'A Case for the Hollow Earth Theory' in *Nexus* magazine, December 1994:

> There is a special characteristic of centrifugal force and we must not overlook this important fact. The strength of 'c-force' becomes greatly lessened as it approaches right angles to the direction of spin. A simple day-to-day example of this behaviour is water in a basin. If you remove the drain plug and allow the water to start emptying from the basin, what will you

eventually observe? A vortex or whirlpool, an empty space surrounded by rapidly rotating material.

Now imagine this same principle concerning the contradicting body which was to become our Earth. At right angles to the rotational axis—in other words, the poles—the 'c-force' was considerably weaker than elsewhere, especially the equator. Therefore, although at the Earth's equator the 'c-force' was able to halt the material's inward progress at about an 8,000 mile diameter, it was considerably less successful in the polar regions, there stopping the contraction at about 1,400 miles. The inevitable outcome of this natural compromise is that our planet concluded its evolution as an 8,000-mile hollow sphere with 1,400 mile-diameter polar openings.

As a result of their study of astronomical records and photographs of nebulae and comets, Harp and other researchers have determined that at the precise centre of these translucent spheres is a proportionately small incandescent ball. The large intervening space indicates that the nebula is also hollow, with the bright sphere at its centre. This phenomenon, they believe, also occurs in the Hollow Earth. For if the Earth was at one time a ball of fire and molten metal, some of this fire would remain at its centre while the centrifugal force caused the rest of the matter to form a solid crust. The Hollow Earth would thereby gain a 'fiery ball' or sun at its centre.

Again this can be demonstrated in a very straightforward way. We know that, apart from at the poles, the centrifugal force of Earth is at its weakest in the precise centre. This can be put to the test by sprinkling some white powder on the surface of a long-playing record. As the record spins, the powder will be hurled to the edge of its surface—with the exception of a tiny proportion left intact at the centre.

Thus we can see how the central sun probably came into existence to provide the inner world with light, heat and the energy to sustain all forms of life.

Another theory about the Hollow Earth suggests this sun might be powered by nuclear fission rather than fusion like stars. It would only need to be a couple of hundred miles in diameter to weigh millions of tons and give enough light to the interior world. And because of its nuclear nature, this little globe would generate a magnetic field just like the Sun.

Seismologists, of course, prefer the explanation that the Earth's core is *liquid*, the argument being that certain waves can only travel through solid materials and not through liquids, gases or a vacuum. There have been differing views in the scientific community about this, however, especially in a suggestion that even if the core of the Earth is a molten ball, the mantle or overlying mass of rock must have two distinct zones, one nearer the core where heat and pressure put the solid rock in a state of 'flowage', and an upper zone where 'fracture' can occur. The depth of this upper zone is the crucial point of the debate.

Professor Frank D. Adams of Montreal University demonstrated not long ago by actual experiment that empty cavities might exist in granite at a depth of eleven miles, and his conclusions have been supported by the mathematician Louis V. King, who calculated that at normal temperature a cavity could exist at depths down to between 17.2 and 20.9 miles. The recently discovered 16 'Rous Belts', which give planes of fracture completely penetrating the globe, offer additional support for the possibility.

Another Hollow Earth researcher, Jan Lamprecht, is, however, prepared to go much further in the discussion, as he explained recently in correspondence with the author:

Scientists simply 'assume' that the core is a liquid—
they do not explore the possibility that the core is a

gas or even a vacuum. I have discovered that approximately 7,000 miles from an earthquake you will find a 'shadow' area where certain types of waves never appear. Could the core/hollow be blocking out these waves? Then at about 10,000 miles or so these waves reappear. I also realised the complexity of such waves and how they are reflected and saw that it is quite easy to misinterpret them.

In fact our methods of watching seismic waves leave much to be desired. When waves come up we have no idea where they were—we really can't tell much. But look carefully and you can see a great many waves bouncing off the 'mantle'—we are told this is due to a change in density. Keep in mind that a hollow object makes the wave movements many times more complex because waves bounce back and forth between the two thin crusts and this will complicate the hell out of the whole thing . . . the earth sometimes 'vibrates' for an hour or two after a big quake.

Researchers into the Hollow Earth enigma have also cited a number of other anomalies which add to the mystery. Polar explorers, for example, have for generations commented on the unexpectedly warmer temperatures found in the most extreme northerly and southerly latitudes. Some of these temperatures have been calculated at anything up to 30 degrees warmer than they should be if the Sun were the sole source of heat. The researchers have also found it difficult to accept the scientific explanation that it is warm equatorial air which is heating the poles—especially at such temperatures after the distance it has travelled. Warm air rising from the Hollow Earth sun is their preferred explanation.

The huge numbers of fish in the polar regions, far denser than in warmer areas, are another element in the puzzle; and it is hard to explain why birds and animals travel north for the winter unless they are seeking the warmth of the inner world. And just add to these the unpredictable behaviour of radio-waves at the North and South Poles; a gravitational increase measurable at the polar curve which is sufficient to cause a marked segregation of salt water and fresh water; and the stones, bits of wood, dust, pollen and mud frequently observed on icebergs which are, of course, composed of *fresh* water and which, despite the lack of annual rain to replace them, every year drift away to melt in their thousands on the polar seas.

There are two further anomalies, one concerning the poles and the other the beautiful auroras associated with them. The fact is that there is no *actual* North or South Pole— no single point on the map, that is, as tradition would have us believe. Both are merely 90 degrees latitude, and because it is assumed the earth is a sphere it is also *assumed* that only one spot in each hemisphere can provide a reading of 90 degrees latitude by the Sun (or any other heavenly body). The eccentric behaviour of compasses in very high latitudes (above the 80th parallel), and the needle showing a vertical movement as the conflicting forces of magnetism and gravity manifest themselves, are both well known experiences. According to the Hollow Earth tradition, it is quite possible to travel into one of the polar openings by accident at a skew angle, remain 'upright' and journey for several hundred miles in and out again and never know you have been there. The fact that gravity is working as normal enables the traveller to remain 'upright' even when, in relation to the outside world, he is upside down. Everything else, including the atmosphere—approximately 30 miles high as on the outside—the waters and winds would be just as normal, although it is believed there may well be a 'vacuum' at the very centre of both apertures.

The *aurora borealis* and *aurora australis* are phenomena that have fascinated and puzzled mankind for centuries.

These beautiful lights, which are virtually exclusive to the polar regions, assume a variety of shapes from arcs to coronas and mainly appear in different shades of green and red. They are suggested by science to be caused by electrical particles emitted by the Sun striking the atoms of the upper atmosphere. However, they have a quite different explanation within the context of the Hollow Earth theory. According to Albert McDonald, an English researcher who has made a particular study of the phenomenon, they are *actually* caused by the inner world sun. In an essay, 'The Hollow Earth', published in *New Worlds* in 1977, he wrote:

Science has never come forward with a satisfactory explanation for the northern and southern polar lights. They say these magnificent sky lights are possibly caused by electrical or magnetic storms at the poles. But the problem with this theory is that electricity and magnetism do not move about haphazardly, auroras are affected by local weather changes, and while most electrical phenomena like lightning are extremely noisy, they are completely silent. As far as being caused by particles from the Sun, not enough are received in the upper atmosphere to cause this. Moreover, we know that such particles are mainly hydrogen and yet very little of this has been recorded in any spectrograph analysis of auroras. It is also a fact that when viewed at either the North or South Pole they have no effect whatsoever on a compass needle!

A number of people who have investigated the phenomen, myself included, feel the *Borealis* and *Australis* are actually a reflection from the sun in the interior of the earth. There are just too many 'sun-like' particles in the atmosphere over the poles to have come from the Sun alone. The fact is that light from the inner sun is emitted through the polar openings. It bounces off the earth's atmosphere and is reflected back *down* on the icy glare of the polar regions and thus we have those unusual lights.

Jan Lamprecht believes that the auroras are also linked to the Earth's geomagnetic field which he maintains is far from stable. It wobbles a great deal and at a high rate, and can move long distances within a short space of time. All of which, in his estimation, can be explained by the presence of the inner world sun moving around its central point:

The magnetic field of this sun would flow out of the Earth through its holes. As this little sun wobbles around, so would the magnetic field. The magnetic current would flow out of, say, the South Pole across the surface of the Earth and in through the North Pole. A compass on a ship outside would point towards the North. As you got closer to the hole, the compass would begin pointing *down*. If you didn't physically adjust your compass down then it might begin spinning around. As you got deeper into the hole and reached the inner surface, you would find your compass returning to normal again. It would still point 'North' but that would now be 'South'. It is important also to remember that the Earth's motion through space is not perfectly constant. In fact the Earth speeds up and slows down in its motion. Thus our little inner sun would wobble around like a passenger in a bus.

As part of his argument. Lamprecht cites the experience of the Norwegian explorer Fridtjof Nansen who, in 1895, while on board his ship the *Fram* trying to reach the North Pole, lost his bearings and reported seeing a *red sun* at a time when the Sun itself was known to be below the horizon. A number of other polar explorers have similarly glimpsed this 'mock sun' in places where the Sun could not possibly be, the only possible explanation according to Lamprecht being that it was shining through a polar opening.

The most obvious question the reader will ask at this point is why, if the Hollow Earth really exists, these polar openings are not easily visible? The answer is much the same as the explanation of why the eye cannot tell the earth is round: the curve is too gradual to observe. The gradual curve of the huge polar openings is impossible to detect visually; moreover, the whole area is usually obscured by thick layers of cloud which make detection difficult even for circling satellites. Note that I have used the word 'difficult' rather than 'impossible', the reason for which the reader will discover later.

On the basis of these facts, then, it is surely quite wrong to dismiss the Hollow Earth concept out of hand as pure hearsay and supposition. Indeed, the evidence that exists to support the actuality of the subterranean world, the stories of those who have set out to find it—men of learning and scientists as well as eccentrics and well-meaning cranks— and the suggestions as to who might live there, add up to a substantial case and provide a constantly surprising journey through history.

Two

ANCIENT LEGENDS OF
THE HOLLOW VOID

Tory Island lies off the north-west corner of Donegal, about seven miles from the Irish mainland. At first glance it seems a rather desolate-looking place composed of hard siliceous rocks with a thin covering of soil, much of which has long since been eroded by the wildness of the elements. Yet because of its very barrenness and isolation, time seems to have stood still on Tory. And stood still for a very long time indeed.

Due to the angle at which the island faces the dark, heaving Atlantic, the winds and sea are notoriously rough, and sometimes days will pass when small boats cannot make the crossing from Sheep Haven on the mainland. But those visitors who do undertake the journey often return exclaiming that Tory is more intriguing than its famous neighbour, Aran, and more steeped in ancient Irish history than many another place in Ireland.

Like most of the western islands, Tory has no trees and the side facing the Atlantic is bounded by high cliffs of naked rock which have been worn into fantastically shaped pillars or 'tors'. It is these which give the island its name from the Irish *toraigh*, meaning an island abounding with towering rocks. Some of these pillars thrust upwards like great monoliths from a past age, while others seem as if they have been hewn by ancient craftsmen to look like signposts pointing to who knows where beyond the northern horizon.

The eastern end of the island is separated from the larger portion by a narrow neck and is known as the 'dun' (pronounced 'doon'). A number of earthen fortifications are still visible here, and it is believed that a prehistoric fort once stood on the spot. Certainly there was a fortress in the seventeenth century when a group of islanders made their last stand against the forces of the English crown. As Tory lies on the track of the North Atlantic shipping routes, wrecks have often occurred hereabouts, and the evidence is there to see in the pieces of steel, bars of iron and variety of items from sunken ships that have been put to good use in islanders' homes.

Tory Island is a place where ancient legends persist and many stories of bygone eras are still told. The inhabitants tend to live to a ripe old age, and there are accounts of men and women seeking new partners when they are over a hundred years old. In former times they even elected a 'king', and an ornate chair still exists which belonged to the last ruler. Many of the islanders still speak Gaelic, and it is the very survival of this language that has helped to preserve the ancient traditions passed down, orally, from generation to generation since time immemorial.

Writing about this aspect of life on Tory Island, Professor Thomas Westropp, a member of the Royal Irish Academy and an expert on the legendary lands of the Atlantic, noted in the society's journal in October 1953:

It is easy to understand the persistence of tradition and the spoken word in a long-living, primitive and isolated community, and nowhere have I observed this emphasised so strongly as on Tory Island. Prehistoric myths and legends are mixed up with events of medieval history and recent happenings, and the whole jumble is narrated as if it were a single tale of the occurrences of a few years ago. The predominating figure of the mythology of the island is Balor, the Chief of the Fomorians, a race of legendary marauders who inhabited the island in early times and from their stronghold scourged the rest of Ireland with their depredations.

It was a confrontation between these evil Fomorians and a mystical race called the Tuatha Dé Danann, who came to Ireland from a 'land beyond the ocean', according to Robert Charroux in *Lost Worlds: Scientific Secrets of the Ancients* (1971), that has provided us with one of the earliest stories connected with the Hollow Earth legend.

In Irish legend the Fomorians were a 'misshapen and violent people', and such was their reputation that they became regarded as the evil gods of Irish myth. The most authoritative source of information about them is the *Book of the Dun Cow*, a manuscript written around 1090, which says their first landfall on Ireland was at Tory Island which they made into their chief stronghold. Remnants of their occupation are still to be seen in the form of earthworks, a round tower of irregular blocks of stone, an ancient dolmen and some inscribed stones.

Once the Fomorians had secured their base, they set about attacking and enslaving the other races on the mainland. These included the Partholóns, the Nemedians and the remarkable Tuatha Dé Danann, who were ultimately to prove their undoing. Partholón, the leader of the first group, was a descendant of Magog and with his people settled in Munster where they courageously staved off the attacks of the Fomorians until wiped out by an outbreak of plague. The Nemedians, who came to Ireland from Scythia, fared no better. After years of oppression by the Fomorians— including one famous victory against the Fomorian king,

Conan—they were virtually exterminated by a retaliatory raid which left less than 30 Nemedians alive to flee the country for ever.

The Tuatha Dé Danann, however, were to prove very different adversaries. There has always been much speculation about the true origins of these tall, pale-skinned, handsome men and women who, Irish legend believes, were the people of the goddess Dana and had come to Ireland from a 'beauteous land' in the north. Lucretius, the Roman philosopher who speculated on the origins of the universe in his work, wrote of them, 'For many years among the depths of the earth they led their life,' while Robert Charroux has added even more significantly, 'The Tuatha Dé Danann brought magic objects: the Nuada Sword, the Lug Spear, the Dagde Cauldron, and the Fal Stone, or Stone of Destiny, which cried out when the legitimate king sat on it.'

Unlike the violent Fomorians, the *Book of the Dun Cow* says, the Tuatha were seen as gods of light and goodness. Brave and courageous fighters when the need arose, they sought to establish the same kind of peace and harmony they had enjoyed in their homeland beyond the seas. In this far-off place there were said to be four fabulous cities, Falias, Gorias, Finias and Murias. They were clearly a unique people, and as Peter Berresford Ellis has noted in his *Dictionary of Irish Mythology* (1987), 'When the Christian monks started to write down the sagas, these gods and goddesses were demoted into heroes and heroines, although much remained to demonstrate their godlike abilities.'

Having said this, the Tuatha were not entirely supermen and women. They enjoyed the normal human pursuits of happiness, pleasure and love—and certain kinds of vice were evidently not unknown among the sexes. It was clear, too, that they possessed an intelligence far above the other peoples of the time and were skilled in the use of occult powers which no one else understood, as Lady Wilde mentions in her *Ancient Legends of Ireland* (1888): 'These Tuatha were great necromancers, skilled in all magic, and excellent in all the arts as builders, poets and musicians.'

They were advanced, too, in terms of their knowledge of medicine and science. The story of Nuada, the man who became their first leader on their arrival in Ireland, bears this out. In an early skirmish with the Fomorians one of his hands was severed by an enemy sword. Dian Cécht, described in the old texts as a 'god of medicine', operated on Nuada's arm and provided a fully operational metal replacement. This artificial limb earned the leader his enduring epithet, 'Nuada of the Silver Hand'.

If there was anyone who could put a stop to the depredations of the Fomorians in their stronghold on Tory Island is was therefore the Tuatha Dé Danann who were an awesome force, according to Lady Wilde: 'A splendid sight was the cavalcade of the Tuatha knights. Seven-score steeds, each with a jewel on his forehead like a star, and seven-score horsemen, all the sons of kings, in their green mantles fringed with gold, and golden helmets on their heads, and golden graves on their limbs, and each knight having in his hand a golden spear.'

The Fomorian hordes were now ruled by a man named Balor of the Evil Eye and had come to believe themselves invincible. Balor, in particular, glorified in his nickname— given, it was said, because he had a gaze so malevolent that it could destroy anyone upon whom it fell. However, he was also a deeply superstitious man, and when it was prophesied that he would be killed by his own grandson, Balor ordered the building of a crystal tower on Tory Island in which he imprisoned his only daughter, Ethlinn, so that she might never have a child.

When rumours of this beautiful prisoner reached the ears of Cian, the son of the Tuatha medicine man, Cécht—so the legend goes—he vowed to rescue the girl. Disguised as a woman he managed to fool the guards and reach the girl, but quickly realised he would never be able to smuggle her out of the tower. Instead, he made love to her and crept away before the dawn light broke. When Balor later heard Ethlinn was pregnant he must have realised his worst fears were about to come true.

At the famous Battle of Magh Tuireadh, the Fomorians and Tuatha Dé Danann confronted one another, and although Balor succeeded in slaying the brave Nuada, his forces were soundly beaten. As had been foretold, Balor was afterwards slain by his grandson, Lugh, and with his death the Fomorians' reign of terror in Ireland came to an end. (Interestingly, the evil ruler's name still holds a fascination in Tory Island tradition, and when a small horde of Elizabethan silver was found in 1931 on the 'dun', the woman who made the discovery was convinced it was 'Balor's money'.)

For a time Ireland enjoyed peace and prosperity under the benevolent rule of the Tuatha Dé Danann until another race, the Milesians, came to challenge their authority. These people, originally from Spain, were named after Milesius, meaning 'soldier', who was said to be able to trace his ancestry back to Ancient Egypt. These men are today generally referred to in Irish history as the last group of invaders before the historical period, and the ancestors of the Goidelic Celtic inhabitants of the country. It was the four sons of Milesius, Eber, Amairgen, Ir and Colpa, who carried out the successful conquest of Ireland and the defeat of the Tuatha. At this point our story takes on an even greater air of mystery.

According to most accounts, the surviving Tuatha Dé Danann were driven out of Ireland and returned to their fabulous cities in the north. Could they have been returning to their homeland *inside* the earth? Historians John Michell and Robert J. M. Rickard, in a chapter on the Hollow Earth in their book *Phenomena* (1977), believe the possibility is inescapable:

> If there is any truth in the ancient myths and histories, there must once have been considerable traffic between the lower world and the upper. People moved from one to the other. We recall, for example, that according to the old Irish histories there was once a battle between the Milesians and the magically skilled race, the Tuatha Dé Danann, for possession of the country. Finally, it was split between them, the victorious Milesians taking the upper half and banishing the older race to the country below the surface.

A curious six-foot high 'T' cross standing by the northern seashore is believed by some to bear mute witness to this passing. Although several authorities feel the cross is Christian in origin, a local tradition insists that it is actually of much earlier date. There are suggestions that it bears certain similarities to a type of cross found in Egypt and thereby links this remote corner of Ireland to the desert land half a world away which, as Erich von Däniken suggested, may have its own entranceway to the Hollow Earth. Certainly there is not another like it in Ireland and it carries three strange marks which have so far defied explanation—beyond a theory that the cross was the handiwork of a Tuatha craftsman and the cuts are the result of an attempt by a Milesian to destroy it, which failed because it proved too hard. A final judgement on this supposition awaits further research.

Another tradition claims that the Tuatha Dé Danann went back to their ancestral home through a large, crater-like hole on the northern cliffs of Tory Island. About fifty yards wide at the top, this hole narrows considerably on the way down to the sea which often encroaches into the lower reaches through a gap near the base of the cliffs. Perhaps not surprisingly, the islanders regard the spot with considerable trepidation and many avoid it by night. A few have even claimed to have heard strange noises coming from the hole.

Michell and Rickard have also written that when the Tuatha Dé Danann disappeared 'underground' they became demoted in the eyes of the people and their very existence was soon being merged into the tales of *sheegees* (fairies) and other mythical beings. But is it possible that these mysterious people *were* from the Hollow Earth? Some scholars have suggested they may have been Norsemen, although there is no mention on any map of Scandinavia of the fabulous cities from which they were said to come: Falias, Gorias, Finias and Murias. Nor is there any evidence that the Norse people were as intelligent or as technically advanced, both scientifically and medically, as the Tuatha at this point in their history. But if they *were* from the land beyond the poles as Hollow Earth researchers believe, then they were just the latest in a line of visitors to the surface—as Michell and Rickard suppose—stretching back to the very earliest times.

*   *   *

In the old Konkan kingdom in India a series of cave paintings was discovered in the last century which is said to illustrate a tradition that dates back to prehistory. The pictures show a group of people emerging from a 'hollow void' below the earth's surface and, according to legend, they are the first human beings arriving from the subterranean world to begin populating the Earth.

Two tribes of Native Americans also possess legends that humans originated in the subterranean world. The Mandan Indians believe they once dwelt in a single underground village near a vast lake. A grape vine extended its roots down to their habitation and gave them a view of the light above. Some of the more adventurous men and women climbed up the vine and were amazed with the sight that met their eyes, of an earth covered with buffalo and every kind of vegetation. When about half the nation had ascended this vine, a big or buxom woman who was then clambering up, broke it with her weight and 'closed upon herself and the rest the light of the Sun'.

Among the Sioux Indians also a story is told that they once lived in a huge underworld community before making their way to the surface. The legend says their exit was hastened by a war started by an evil god who was held at bay by a group of Sioux warriors later acknowledged as the gods of good fortune by the tribe.

In the East there is a tradition that Adam himself came from a subterranean world. According to this version of the origin of mankind, Adam's home was 'in the middle of the Earth' and his mission had been to scout the land. Hindu lore adds weight to this legend by saying that Adam was the king of a group who had fled into the Hollow Earth after a great cataclysm and then returned to the surface to re-establish the human race.

Various other ancient religious texts also speak of a world underneath the Earth's crust. When, for instance, Gilgamesh, the legendary hero of the ancient Sumerian and Babylonian epics, went to visit his ancestor Utnapishtim, he descended into the bowels of the Earth. It was there, too, that Orpheus travelled to seek the soul of Euridice. Ulysses, having reached the farthermost boundaries of the western world, offered a sacrifice so that the spirits of the Ancients would rise from the depths of the Earth and give him advice. In some legends, Venus is also said to have been banished 'to the bowels of the Earth'.

Writing of this whole tradition in his *Records of the Past* (1923), genealogist A. M. Sayce says, 'We are often told of a dwelling which ''the gods created'' for the first human beings—a dwelling in which ''they become great'' and ''increase in numbers'' and the location of which is described in words exactly corresponding to those of Indian, Chinese, Eddaic and Aztecan literature, namely, ''in the centre of the earth''.'

Interestingly, a number of such traditions state that the Earth's first civilisation probably began in the far North, before the ice-cap froze the Arctic wastes. They record that man's ancestors appeared from the 'Land of the Gods', 'The Imperishable Isles' and 'Mount Meru', an abode of light and beauty beyond the North Pole and described in one account as 'vaguely extended to the Northern sky'. To the people of antiquity, this region was a wondrous, sacred place inhabited by magicians conjuring the destiny of mankind. Today there is a fascinating echo of these ancient traditions in the fact that children send notes to Father Christmas in his 'wonderland' at the North Pole, asking for gifts.

Hollow Earth researchers have also pointed out a number of quotations from the Bible which, they say, show the concept was well known and understood at that time, especially from the Books of the Ephesians, Isaiah and Job. Most telling of all are the lines from Job 26: 7–10 which, they maintain, refer to the North Pole and the subterranean world that lies below:

He stretcheth out the north over the empty place and hangeth the earth upon nothing.
He bindeth up the waters in his thick clouds; and the cloud is not rent under them.
He holdeth back the face of his throne, and spreadeth his cloud upon it.
He hath encompassed the waters with bounds, until the day and night come to an end.

The Greek philosopher Plato (*c*.427–347 BC) was probably the first man to write at any length on the idea of an underworld. In several of his works he mentions 'enormous subterranean streams' and 'tunnels both broad and narrow in the interior of the earth', and he also discusses those who might dwell there. In one significant paragraph in *Timaeus* he says: 'Apollo's real home is among the Hyperboreans, in a land of perpetual life, where mythology tells us two doves flying from the opposite ends of the world met in this fair region, the home of Apollo. Indeed, according to Hecataeus, Leto, the mother of Apollo, was born on an island in the Arctic Ocean *far beyond the North Wind*' (my italics).

Another remark by Plato is equally intriguing: 'He is the god who sits in the centre, on the navel of the Earth; and he is the interpreter of religion to all mankind.' To Hollow Earth believers, 'the navel of the Earth' is proof positive that the great thinker believed in a subterranean world.

The first man to write an entire work devoted to the concept of the Hollow Earth was, perhaps surprisingly, the English astronomer and mathematician, Edmond Halley (1656–1742). He it was who saw, in 1682, the comet now named after him and ten years later he was appointed Astronomer Royal. Halley was a close friend of Sir Isaac Newton and discussed at length with him the latter's epoch-making *Philosophia Naturalis Principia Mathematica* (1687) from which have derived the mathematical formulae that provide the basis for all modern engineering achievements. But while Halley agreed with his friend's explanations for all manner of phenomena, from the motion of planets to the fall of cannon-shot, he appeared to have no answer for certain anomalies like magnetic variations. Halley had in mind particularly the fact that the world's magnetic poles—those to which compass needles point—wandered about rather than staying in place.

The result of his deliberations was an article, 'An Account of the Cause of the Change of the Variation of the Magnetic Needle; With an Hypothesis of the Structure of the Internal Parts of the Earth', published in the *Philosophical Transactions* of the Royal Society of London in 1692. In this lengthy work, argued with the aid of mathematics and philosophy, he suggested that the Earth was not a solid body but hollow in the middle. It also contained three spheres which, he said, solved the problem of magnetic variations. According to Halley, all one had to assume was that the magnetic poles were really situated on one or both of the inner spheres and that they revolved on their axis at a slightly different speed from that of the Earth's outer crust. The core of Edmond Halley's argument was given in these words:

The External Parts of the Globe may well be reckoned as the Shell, and the Internal as a Nucleus or inner Globe, included within ours, with a fluid Medium between. Which having the same common Centre and Axis of diurnal Rotation, may turn about with our Earth each 24 hours; only this outer Sphere having its turbinating Motion some small matter either swifter or slower than the internal Ball. And a very minute difference in length of time, by many repetitions becoming sensible, the Internal parts will by degrees recede from the External, and not keeping pace with one another, will appear gradually to move either Eastwards or Westwards by the difference of their motions. Now supposing such an Internal Sphere having such a Motion, we shall solve the difficulty. For if this exterior Shell of Earth be a Magnet, having its Poles at a distance from the Poles of Diurnal Rotation; and if the Internal Nucleus be likewise a Magnet, having its Poles in two other Places, distant also from the Axis; and these latter by a gradual and slow Motion change their place in respect

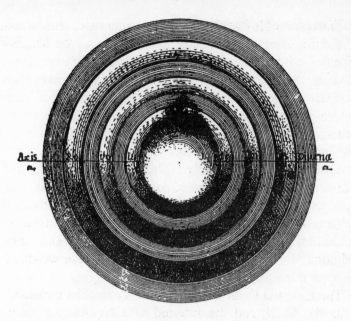

Edmond Halley's diagram of the Hollow Earth, which appeared with
his article in *Philosophical Transactions*

of the External; we may give a reasonable account
of the Needle's Variations which till now hath been
unattempted.

After listing what he believes might be the reader's major
objections to his theory—that no such inner globe would
be able to keep its place in the centre of the shell, that sea
water would constantly leak in, and the constant darkness
inside would make all life impossible—Halley rather lamely
cites 'the wisdom of the Creator to provide for the Macro-
cosm by many more ways than I can either imagine or
express'. He does, though, include a diagram of his vision
of the Hollow Earth along with some mathematical figures
to explain his concept:

I adjoin the following Scheme, wherein the Earth is

represented by the outward Circle, and the three inward Circles are made nearly proportionable to the Magnitudes of the planets *Venus*, *Mars* and *Mercury*, all of which may be included within the Globe of Earth, and all the Arches more than sufficiently strong to bear their Weight. The concave of each Arch, which is shaded differently from the rest, I suppose to be made up of Magnetical Matter and the whole to turn about the same common Axis only with this difference, that the Outer Sphere still moves somewhat faster than the Inner. Thus the Diameter of the Earth being about eight thousand English Miles, I allow five hundred Miles for the thickness of its Shell, and another space of five hundred Miles for a Medium between, capable of an immense Atmosphere for the use of the globe of *Venus*: *Venus* again I give a shell of the same thickness, and leave as great a space between her Concave and *Mars*; so likewise from *Mars* to *Mercury*, which latter Ball we will suppose solid and about two thousand Miles Diameter.

Halley concluded his paper with a challenge: 'Thus I have showed a possibility of a much more ample Creation than has hitherto been imagined; and if this seem strange to those that are unacquainted with the Magnetical System, it is hoped that all such will endeavour, first, to inform themselves of the Matter of Fact, and then try if they can find out a more simple Hypothesis.'

Sir Edmond Halley's theory of the Hollow Earth went into several editions and revisions during the next 30 years, suggesting that it was probably known to the literate general public although it does not appear to have been well received by his scientific contemporaries. Most of them were more interested in his ideas about the deviations of the magnetic needle. Nonetheless, the Astronomer Royal continued to defend his theory, adding a further significant comment in March 1716 after a spectacular display of the *aurora borealis* was seen throughout northern Europe. To Halley this provided the answer to *what* illuminated the subterranean world. He wrote another paper for the *Philosophical Transactions* in which he described the display in detail and offered an explanation.

According to Halley, the various ideas which had been put forward by astronomers about the origin of the phenomenon were quite inadequate. He had reached the conclusion that the lights were caused by 'an escape of the luminous material which gives the eternal spheres perpetual daylight'. This material, he said, would naturally escape where the outer sphere was thinnest—which was, of course, the far north, for his friend Newton had just shown that the earth was flattened at the poles—and he believed the flattening was due to a thinning of the outer sphere.

Although, subsequently, mathematicians and physicists in general dismissed Halley's statement, there were a number of other men intrigued enough by the concept to make mention of it in their own works. Among the first of these was Cotton Mather (1663–1728), the New England Puritan clergyman famous for inciting the Salem witchcraft mania, who agreed wholeheartedly with the concept and repeated what Halley had written almost verbatim in a chapter 'On Magnetism' in his *The Christian Philosopher* (1721). 'We may reckon the extreme Parts of our Globe as a *Shell*,' he wrote, 'the internal as a *Nucleus*, or an *Inner Globe* included within ours; and between these a *Fluid Medium*, which having the same common Centre and Axis of diurnal Rotation, may turn about our Earth every four and twenty hours.'

In a later section, Mather stated that he was also in agreement with Halley's conclusion about the *aurora borealis*: 'The inner medium itself may be always luminous; or the concave Arch may shine with such a Substance as does invest the Surface of the Sun; or they may have a peculiar *Luminaries*, whereof we can have no idea . . . But it is time to stop, we are got beyond *Human Penetration*; we have dug as far as 'tis fit any *Conjecture* should carry us!'

Despite Mather's unabashed repetition of Halley's work, it is probably true to say that he helped to keep the Hollow Earth idea alive when later generations of readers, consulting his works for their accounts of devils, demons and all manner of other strange manifestations, came across the relevant chapter.

The prolific Swiss mathematician Leonhard Euler (1707–1783) who developed new methods of solving problems in observational astronomy, later argued that if the earth was hollow there could only be *one* interior world with a central sun to provide illumination. By contrast, Sir John Leslie (1766–1832), the Scottish natural philosopher and experimenter in radiation, felt this inner world more likely to have *two* suns revolving around a common centre of gravity. He even named them Pluto, after the Greek god of the underworld, and Prosperine, the demi-goddess who was his wife for half of each year.

Despite the comments of all these men, and the public curiosity, it was to be almost a century before anyone again tackled the Hollow Earth enigma with the same dedication as Sir Edmond Halley. This time, however, the proponent was a man not merely content with expounding a *theory* as the Astronomer Royal had done, but also an adventurer who set his heart on actually *visiting* the subterranean world that he was convinced lay beneath his feet.

Three

THE THEORY OF
CONCENTRIC SPHERES

Standing in an old park in Hamilton in south-western Ohio
is a curious, weatherbeaten monument which is easy to miss
in the everyday bustle of the industrial city. It is made of
a four-sided shaft almost five feet high and surmounted by
a hollow sphere. The inscription below, worn or defaced
almost to the point of illegibility, informs anyone who stops
to look that it was erected in 1829 by a man with the curious
name of Americus Vespucius Symmes, to commemorate
the life of his father, Captain John Cleaves Symmes. The
memorial honours him not as a soldier, for the city boasts
a magnificent Soldiers, Sailors and Pioneers Monument, but,
far more remarkably, as the first modern champion of the
Hollow Earth legend. The words on the plaque are as odd
as any to be found on a monument anywhere in the world:

CAPTAIN JOHN CLEVES SYMMES
Soldier, Philosopher and the originator of
Symmes' Theory of Concentric Spheres and Polar Voids
He contended the Earth was Hollow and Habitable Within

Sadly, little is known by most people in Hamilton about
Symmes' life or his theory. Those who do acknowledge the
Captain tend to regard him as an eccentric who wore himself
out vainly touring the country lecturing people on his crack-
pot theories and trying to win support for an expedition to

the inner world. Yet what Symmes did, following a distinguished career as a soldier, was to devote himself with single-minded determination to explaining what he believed to be the answer to the age-old question of the Hollow Earth.

The city of Hamilton lies on the Great Miami River about 25 miles north of Cincinnati and manufactures textiles, paper, automobile parts, safes, and mechanical and hydraulic presses. Despite being the seat of local government, it could never be described as a tourist attraction, although it does have a rather curious history. The first building here was Fort Hamilton, which was used between 1791 and 1796 by General 'Mad' Anthony Wayne as his base for fighting the Indians. In 1794 a town called Fairfield was built alongside the fort, and this was later renamed after Alexander Hamilton, the American statesman. With the construction in the mid-1850s of the Miami and Erie Canal, providing connections to Cincinnati in the south and Dayton to the north, its future as a centre was assured.

The early settlers in this part of Ohio probably had other things on their minds than the investigation of the enormous mounds to be seen all over the area which, according to legend, had been there since ancient times. Certainly, those who farmed the land, with more practical considerations to worry about, levelled many of them to the ground before any archaeologists had a chance to carry out research. It is no part of our history to speculate on the actual origins of the mounds, but Robert Charroux has one fascinating theory to offer in his book *The Mysterious Unknown* (1972):

In North America, and especially in Ohio, mounds and enormous serpentines are found which were built of earth before the dawn of even prehistoric times. There is no doubt that in the olden days they existed in their thousands—which might make one wonder if the real

'Land of the Hills' of our Celtic ancestors was perhaps not in Mexico but in North America, at least in the very earliest times. Later on perhaps the 'Land of the Hills' may have been in Mexico, when the first earthen tumuli were raised. Whatever the truth may be, the number of artificial mounds in the USA is legion. At Chillicothe, Ohio [not far from Hamilton] there are twenty-four of them, conical in shape . . .

All this seems to make Hamilton, Ohio, a very appropriate spot to be associated with the career of John Cleves Symmes, advocate of the *Theory of Concentric Spheres*, although he was not actually born there but in Sussex County, New Jersey, on 5 November, 1780, and was baptised after a famous uncle of the same name who played a significant role in the history of the mid-West, devising the 'Symmes Purchase'. His predecessors also included a distinguished line of New England clergymen, the earliest being Zachariah Symmes, an English Puritan who had emigrated to Massachusetts from East Anglia in 1634.

At school young John proved adept at mathematics and science and was also an omnivorous reader. As the family library contained a number of the works of Cotton Mather, who had been a friend and fellow clergyman of Zachariah Symmes, it is believed that he first discovered the theory of the Hollow Earth in the pages of *The Christian Philosopher*.

However, at the age of 20, Symmes chose the army as his career and quickly proved himself a capable and efficient soldier. By the year 1812, when the war between America and Great Britain had broken out, he had risen to the rank of Captain. He took part in the battles of Bridgwater and Lundy's Lane and was mentioned for bravery. In 1813 he played an important role in Oliver Hazard Perry's victory at the Battle of Lake Erie, when he led a band of commandos against the British defences, leaving them vulnerable to

Perry's main onslaught. The Captain received several medals for bravery and became something of a hero. Unfortunately, however, his highly individual style of soldiering—which had, nevertheless, helped to make his surprise attack so successful—coupled with his sharp tongue directed at both his men and his superiors, did not endear him to those in command. After the final decisive victory by Andrew Jackson at New Orleans in January 1815, Symmes found himself assigned to a backwoods fort on the Upper Mississippi River.

Although he must have been frustrated at this posting, Symmes decided to make use of his time by developing his interest in how the earth had been formed—inspired all those years before by Cotton Mather's essay. His reading led him to the theories of two American professors, Abner Burnett and John Woodward. Burnett maintained that the Earth had started its existence as a floating mudball covered with oil and picked up 'space rubbish' to form its outer crust; while Woodward suggested the planet was made of distinct layers of different strata that had been laid one upon another, 'like the layers of an onion'. John Cleves Symmes, however, came to his own conclusion—that the earth was hollow with five concentric spheres inside the outer surface, all with a common centre.

Apart from reading scientific works, Symmes had also noticed that in nature many things were hollow; from the reeds growing along the Mississippi river bank to the bones in the meat served at dinner. More controversially, he came to the conclusion that Newton's theory of gravity was *wrong*. Instead he decided the atmosphere was filled with an invisible substance which he named 'Aerial Elastic Fluid', composed of tiny spheres of ether which were also hollow. It was this invisible substance that pushed down against the earth rather than Newton's theory of a 'pulling' process, he maintained.

The whole concept gradually became an obsession with Symmes, and in 1816 he resigned his commission to put his theories to the American public. In order to fund his research he moved to St Louis, Missouri, and set up a trading post where he supplied the military, traded with the Indians, and still found time to work on his project. He also married a widow, Mary Anne Lockwood, who already had six children, and promptly fathered four more, all of whom were given names similar to the firstborn, Americus Vespucius Symmes.

One day, while sitting by the Missouri, another thought occurred to Symmes. If there were entrances to this hollow world the most likely place for them must surely be the North and South Poles. But how to get there and find out? He knew it was imperative to seek the support of government and scientific circles and so he decided to issue a statement. This would go to the US President, to Congress, the major American universities, the heads of state and leading scientists in Europe, as well as to every major town and city in the country. An example of this unique document which ensured Symmes' notoriety, dated 10 April, 1818, still survives in the Library of Congress in Washington, from which I made the following copy:

CIRCULAR

TO ALL THE WORLD
'Light gives light to light discover *ad infinitum*'

St Louis, Missouri Territory,
North America, April 10, 1818.

I declare that the earth is hollow, habitable within; containing a number of solid concentrick spheres; one within the other, and it is open at the poles twelve or sixteen degrees. I pledge my life in support of this truth, and am ready to explore the hollow if the world will support and aid me in the undertaking.

John Cleves Symmes of Ohio,
Late Captain of Infantry.

N.B. I have ready for the press a treatise in the principles of Matter, wherein I show proofs of the above proposition, account for various phenomina [sic], and disclose Dr Darwin's 'Golden Secret'.

My terms are the patronage of this and the new world, I dedicate to my wife and her ten children.

I select Dr S. L. Mitchell, Sir H. Davy and Baron Alexander Von Humboldt as my protectors. I ask one hundred brave companions, well equipped, to start from Siberia, in the fall season, with reindeer and sledges, on the ice of the frozen sea. I engage we will find a warm and rich land, stocked with thrifty vegetables and animals, if not men, on reaching one degree northward of latitude 82; we will return in the succeeding spring.

J. C. S.

Attached to the circular is a note to the effect that the document was accompanied by another letter signed by several prominent citizens of St Louis, testifying that the author was 'a good father, a respected businessman and a Christian gentleman'. However, all that the missive elicited from its recipients was a bemused silence—although, according to some US sources, the Czar of Russia was said to have been intrigued by the idea of new lands to conquer. In Paris, at the Academie des Sciences, the Comte de Volnay dismissed the writer as 'a madman'.

Undeterred, Symmes wrote a number of newspaper articles about his theory and decided to give lectures at which he would appeal for donations to fund the expedition. A young man, Paul Clark, who was present at one of the Captain's lectures to the faculty and students of Union College in the winter of 1826–7, took copious notes and later wrote an invaluable article, 'The Symmes Theory of the Earth', which appeared in the *Atlantic Monthly* of April 1873. In this he writes:

According to his theory, the earth is globular, hollow, and open at the poles. The diameter of the northern opening is about two thousand miles, of four thousand miles from outside to outside. The southern opening is somewhat larger. The planes of these openings are parallel to each other, but form an angle of 12 degrees with the equator, so that the highest part of the north plane is directly opposite the lowest part of the south plane. The shell of the earth is about one thousand miles thick, and the edges of this shell at the opening are called verges, and measure, from the regular concavity within to the regular convexity without, about fifteen hundred miles. The verges occupy about 25 degrees, and if delineated on a map would show only the outer half of the verge, while all above or farther from the equator, both north and south, would lie on the apex and within the verge. All the polar regions upon the present map would be out of sight. The meridian lines extend at right angles from the equator to the outer edges of the verges, and then wind round along the surface of the verges, terminating at the points directly under the highest parts of the verges both north and south.

The line which marks the location of the apex of the northern verge begins at a point in Lapland about 68 degrees N and 20 degrees E from London on a meridian traversing Spitzbergen, whence it passes southwest across the Atlantic Ocean and the southern part of Greenland, through Hudson's Bay and over the continent to the Pacific near Cook's Inlet, thence across the Fox Islands, to a point about 56 degrees N and 160 degrees W nearly south of the Bering Straits. Then it passes over the Pacific, crossing the south part of Kamtchatka, continuing northwest through Siberia, entering Europe across the Ural Mountains, in latitude about 58 degrees N and passing near the Arctic coast, over the mouth of the White Sea, to the point of starting . . .

Captain Symmes collated with great labour many isolated facts from his own researches, and from the accounts of Ross, Howe, Parry, McKenzie and others who had by land and sea explored the polar regions, while similar proofs have been drawn from later explorations since the promulgation of the theory in 1829. The explorers who furnish facts for the support of this theory seem, none of them, to have had the remotest conjecture of it. The facts are admitted and it cannot be urged against the author that he has marshalled in its support fictitious premises.

As part of his argument, says Clark, Symmes cited the remarkable differences in climate experienced at the poles; the vast open areas of ocean that exist there; phenomena like the *aurora borealis* which could only be explained by light coming through polar openings; the erratic behaviour of magnetic needles; and, finally, the rings of Saturn as proof of the theory of concentricity in nature. The Captain had amassed an impressive collection of facts and arguments to support his theory, his attentive listener concluded, and 'only time the great revealer of secrets will determine whether this startling theory is true in whole or in part and whether its author was a visionary or a profound philosopher whose name will be honoured among men.'

Despite the sympathetic hearing John Cleves Symmes received on this occasion, he was often greeted with derision and sometimes even had to physically eject some of the more vigorous hecklers. His rather jingoistic claim that the discovery of the Hollow Earth would bring acclaim to America along with new territories did, however, find a response from audiences in some of the smaller communities of the nation. His appeals for support also caught the attention of a wealthy businessman, James McBride of Miami in Ohio, who was a trustee of the local university and a man with friends in high places. He helped the former soldier with financial aid to settle in nearby Hamilton and there introduced him to the aptly named Richard Mentor Johnson, the Representative of the adjoining state of Kentucky. Johnson proved to be an open-minded, intelligent politician who, although not altogether convinced by Symmes' theory, felt it at least deserved an airing in Washington.

Consequently, on 28 January, 1823, Johnson proposed in Congress that 'The US Government finance an expedition to claim the lands inside the earth.' He outlined Symmes' theory and his plans and held up a huge sheaf of letters which he claimed had come from people in Ohio, Kentucky, Indiana and Missouri. 'They are all from sane, intelligent voters demanding that we bring great honour and profit to the United States by opening up these new lands,' he declared.

Sadly, very few of the other representatives shared Johnson's enthusiasm for the proposal and it was shelved. For Symmes it meant looking elsewhere to raise the necessary funds; while for Johnson the moment would soon become no more than just a bizarre incident in a career which would culminate in his being elected Vice-President.

Nevertheless, thanks to the continued support of James McBride, Symmes was able to go on with his punishing

Symmes' terrestrial globe, as represented on the back cover of the 1885 edition of his book, *The Symmes Theory of Concentric Spheres*.

tour of lectures which kept him away from his wife and family in Hamilton for months on end as he criss-crossed the country. In March 1824 he was encouraged by a benefit performance at the Cincinnati Theatre in aid of his proposed expedition, and this was followed two months later by the most successful of all his lectures—in Hamilton, no less. At the end of it the audience passed a resolution 'that we esteem Symmes' Theory of the Earth deserving of serious attention and worthy of the attention of the American people.' McBride saw to the collecting of all Symmes' notes and articles and published them in 1826 as *Symmes' Theory of Concentric Spheres*. The wealthy philanthropist also included an illustration of Symmes' terrestrial globe and a foreword to the book in which he reaffirmed his belief:

Although the particular location of the places where the verges of the polar openings are believed to exist may not have been ascertained with absolute certainty, yet they are believed to be nearly correct. Their localities have been ascertained from appearances that exist in these regions—such as a belt or zone surrounding the globe where trees and other vegetation (except moss) do not grow; the tides of the ocean flowing in different directions and appearing to meet; the ground swells in the sea being more frequent and the *Aurora Borealis* appearing to the southward.

Further petitions for financial aid on Symmes' behalf were sent to Congress and the General Assembly of Ohio, though with a continued lack of success. In 1825 the Captain was granted permission to join a Russian polar expedition but was unable to accept due to his impoverished financial condition and declining health. The strain on his constitution of the strenuous lecture tours finally led to his collapse in the winter of 1828, while he was travelling in Canada. The ever-faithful McBride arranged for him to be transported home to Hamilton, and there he was lovingly cared for by his long-suffering wife. But his obsession with the Hollow Earth ultimately cost John Cleves Symmes his life and he died in his sleep on 29 May, 1829. He was buried with full military honours and his obituary in the *Hamilton Eagle* spoke more admiringly of his army career than of his theory of concentric globes.

But Symmes' theory did not die with him. One of his followers, Joseph Reynolds, a graduate of Ohio University who had been attracted to the Captain after hearing one of his lectures and became his manager responsible for setting up his lectures, decided to carry on trying to raise money for the Hollow Earth expedition. The speeches which he delivered were rather more colourful than those of his mentor, promising a subterranean world flooded with warm light, pleasant cities and, for good measure, a race of 20-foot giants who guarded a priceless treasure. Invitations that Reynolds extended to join the expedition nonetheless raised hundreds of dollars from the public.

Reynolds' greatest triumph was to convince the US Secretary of the Navy, Samuel Lewis Southard, of the viability of the plan. Southard, in turn, appears to have convinced no less a person than the President, John Quincy Adams, that the theory *was* worth investigating, and there is evidence that the President asked for a feasibility study to be made for sending a navy ship to the South Pole. Before this order could be implemented, however, Adams' turn of office came to an end and his successor, the no-nonsense former US commander and hero of the War of 1812, Andrew Jackson (1767–1845), scuppered the proposal.

Joseph Reynolds tried one more scheme. In 1829 he set up the Hollow Earth Exploration Company and issued stock certificates on the New York Stock Exchange. There was, it seemed, something about the idea which appealed to the more adventurous and wealthy people in the city, and with rumours of the fortunes that might be made by finding the subterranean world, Reynolds and his associates raised enough cash to commission two vessels to sail to the South Pole. Both were brigantines: the *Annawan*, commanded by Captain N. B. Palmer, and the *Seraph*, skippered by Captain Robert Pendelton. They sailed from New York harbour on 29 October, 1829.

There is, however, some doubt as to whether Joseph Reynolds actually left on this expedition, although documents show the presence on the *Seraph* of a 'scientist' named 'J. Reynolds' accompanied by one 'Dr Watson'. Equally uncertain is what happened to the two ships. One story maintains that the brigs got no nearer their goal than the coast of Chile before the crews mutinied. Another says the expedition was shipwrecked, while a third has it that they *did* reach the South Pole, but that there a group of seamen put ashore on the ice cap soon got lost and were only rescued just in time to prevent them dying of cold and starvation. What is beyond doubt is that the ill-fated expedition did not find a polar opening and Joseph Reynolds was never heard of again.

It was a tragedy that Symmes' undoubtedly serious intentions should have ended in such a tawdry fashion. But just as his memorial in Hamilton has survived the passage of time, so his idea has continued to inspire others. In the world of literature, too, his theory has generated a veritable library of novels and stories that for a century and a half have intrigued and delighted readers, most of whom probably know little or nothing of their source of inspiration.

Fellow American Edgar Allan Poe virtually invented this school of fiction in his short story 'MS Found in a Bottle' (1833), followed by the novel *The Narrative of Arthur Gordon Pym* (1838) which was unfinished at his death and later 'completed' by Jules Verne who entitled the work *An Antarctic Mystery* (1898). Verne had earlier written probably the best known book on the theme, *Journey to the Centre of the Earth* (1872), about a group of explorers who venture into a hollow earth through the core of a dormant volcano. In 1959 it was intelligently scripted and filmed starring James Mason as the party leader.

The spirit of Symmes is also to be found in William R. Bradshaw's *The Goddess of Atvatabar: Being the History of the Discovery of the Interior Worlds and Conquest of Atvatabar* (1892), which was published complete with a map of the 'Interior World' clearly based on the Captain's own design. This Hollow Earth, however, is peopled by a love cult whose devotees regard sex without orgasm as the way to perpetual youth. *Underground Man* (1896) by Gabriel Tarde found favour with H. G. Wells who provided a preface for the English edition. It describes how the last people on Earth withdraw to a utopian subterranean world when the sun's energy becomes exhausted. Fred Thorpe's short story 'In the World Below' (1897), about adventures in the Hollow Earth, anticipated the famous Pellucidar series

William R. Bradshaw's map of the 'Interior World', which was based on Symmes' concept

of novels by Edgar Rice Burroughs which began with *At the Earth's Core* (1914).

Lost races living in a subterranean world are featured in Charles Willing Beale's popular *The Secret of the Earth* (1899); *Neequa, or The Problem of the Ages* (1900) by Jack Adams, in which sexual equality has been achieved below ground; and Frank Powell's exceedingly rare *The Wolf Men: A Tale of Amazing Adventures in the Underworld* (1906), set in prehistoric times. More recently, S. Fowler Wright has continued the tradition in his *The World Below* (1953), as have Howard Waldrop and Steven Utley in their ingenious short story 'Black as the Pit, from Pole to Pole' (1977), which actually features Symmes, Reynolds and Poe. *The Hollow Earth* (1990) by Rudy Rucker who is Professor of Mathematics at San José State University, has drawn liberally on the entire Symmes saga to describe how his protagonists accidentally stumble into one of the holes at the South Pole as described by the Captain and there find a subterranean world full of more surprises than anyone could possibly imagine.

But the *true* story of the search for the Hollow Earth has its own, even stranger twists and turns, as we shall discover in the next chapter.

Four

THE STRANGE VOYAGE
OF OLAF JANSEN

Today there is no one in Glendale, the sprawling northern suburb of Los Angeles, who is quite sure where Olaf Jansen lived—if they have heard of the remarkable old seaman at all. Years ago, there were some residents who thought that the man who claimed to have travelled into the Hollow Earth had a house close to what is now the Colorado Boulevard, while others had heard that he lived not far from the LA Zoo—which, the cynics said, is where he should have been confined after details of his Münchhausen-like adventures were made public. In all probability, though, his modest little bungalow was not far from Foothill Boulevard in the south-east San Fernando Valley, for Jansen spoke frequently of the view from his bedroom window of the sun rising over the peaks of the San Jacinto range to the east.

Glendale is a busy residential and industrial area with its own airport, college and 600-acre Brand Park. Historically, its main claims to fame are Casa Adobe, an adobe building which dates from the 1860s, and the Forest Lawn Memorial Park where many of the great and good of Los Angeles are laid to rest. The cemetery was created in 1886 on the site of a 1784 Spanish land grant and contains reproductions of a number of great works of art, including the 'Wee Kirk o' the Heather', a facsimile of Scotland's church of Annie

Laurie. Although some reports say that Olaf Jansen is also buried in Forest Lawn, his grave has never been found.

The story told by the old Scandinavian-born sailor of his voyage into the Hollow Earth has been the subject of considerable debate since it was first made public in 1908. Dismissed as a romantic fantasy in some quarters, accused of being a clever adaptation of the theories of John Cleves Symmes in others, Olaf Jansen, then in his nineties, insisted that his narrative was *true* in every respect. Although reluctant to discuss the events for many years because of the initial reaction they generated and the traumatic effect this had upon his life, his testimony is one of the few accounts of a visit to the inner world that has failed to be totally dismissed amid all the welter of Symmes-inspired fiction. By his own admission, Jansen had never even heard of the 'Theory of Concentric Spheres', let alone read anything by or about Symmes, when his strange experience at the North Pole occurred. The facts about his background, and that of the man who later published his story, are well documented.

Olaf Jansen was born on 27 October, 1811 at Uleaborg— now called Oulu—a fishing port on the eastern coast of the Gulf of Bothnia in Finland. His father, Jens Jansen, was Norwegian, having been born on the Lofoten Islands, while his mother came from Stockholm where the couple had made their home. Despite the advanced stage of Mrs Jansen's pregnancy, they had not been deterred from taking their annual cruise in Jens' boat in the Gulf. The Jansens had planned to be back in Stockholm before the birth of their first child, but stormy seas delayed the return trip and made it necessary to head for Uleaborg when Mrs Jansen went into labour. There a baby boy was delivered and it was evident from his size and weight that the infant had inherited his father's height, sturdiness and alert grey eyes. He would also grow up to display the same characteristics of endurance, ruggedness and fierce determination, coupled with a great gentleness.

Young Olaf soon showed that he shared his father's love of the sea. After being educated at a private school in Stockholm until he was fourteen, the boy started to go on regular fishing trips with him around the Scandinavian coast. Jens Jansen was a man who relished the challenge of the sea, but never underestimated its powers. He instructed his son in good seamanship and also filled his head with tales of the legendary Norse gods whom he greatly admired. Olaf Jansen was just nineteen when he and his father set off on the voyage that was to earn them a place in the history of Hollow Earth lore.

According to Olaf Jansen, they left Stockholm in his father's fishing sloop on 3 April, 1829. They sailed southward between the islands of Gotland and Oland, then made their way through the sound which separates Sweden and Denmark. After briefly stopping at Kristiansand on the Norwegian coast, they headed north past the Lofoten Islands before putting in at the most northerly port, Hammerfest. After reprovisioning, father and son sailed on to Spitzbergen, getting their first view of some towering icebergs, before anchoring safely at Wijade Bay on 23 June. Here they fished successfully for several days and then went on through the Hinlopen Strait in the direction of Franz Josef Land. Olaf Jansen takes up the story at this point:

> For several days we sailed along the rocky coast of Franz Josef Land. Finally, a favouring wind came up that enabled us to make the West Coast, and, after sailing for 24 hours, we came to a beautiful inlet. One could hardly believe it was the far Northland. The place was green with growing vegetation, and while the area did not comprise more than one or two acres, yet the

air was warm and tranquil. In front of us and directly
to the north, lay an open sea.

My father was an ardent believer in Odin and Thor,
and had frequently told me there were gods who came
from far beyond the 'North Wind'. There was a tradition, he explained, that still farther northward was a
land more beautiful than mortal man had ever known.
My youthful imagination was fired by the ardour, zeal
and religious fervour of my good father, and I
exclaimed, 'Why not sail to this land? The sky is fair,
the wind is favourable and the sea open.' Even now I
can see the expression of pleasurable surprise on his
countenance as he turned toward me and asked, 'My
son, are you willing to go with me and explore—to go
far beyond where man has ever ventured?' I answered
affirmatively. 'Very well,' he replied. 'May the god
Odin protect us!' and quickly adjusting the sails, he
glanced at our compass, turned the prow in a due northerly direction through an open channel, and our voyage
began.

For three days the fishing sloop continued to sail north until
Olaf was awakened from sleep by the sounds of a fierce
storm and his father calling for help in lowering the sails.
All around their vessel, the young man recalled, was 'a
vapourish fog or mist, black as Egyptian night, and white
like a steam-cloud towards the top, which was finally lost
to view as it blended with the great white flakes of falling
snow.'

As the two seamen wrestled with the sails, the boat
pitched and rolled as if in the grip of a whirlpool. This
ordeal continued for three hours until the two drenched and
exhausted sailors found themselves in calm waters. As they
checked over the boat for any signs of damage, Olaf suddenly noticed a peculiar phenomenon above them:

The sun was beating down slantingly, as if we were in a southern latitude, instead of in the far Northland. It was swinging around, its orbit ever visible and rising higher and higher, frequently mist-covered, yet always peering through the lacework of clouds like some fretful eye of fate, guarding the mysterious Northland. Far to our right, the rays catching the icebergs provided a pyrotechnic panorama of countless colours and shapes; while below could be seen the green-tinted sea, and above, the purple sky.

When Olaf accidentally tasted some drops of sea water on his hand, he was amazed to discover that it was *fresh* water. After replenishing their supplies with this unexpected piece of good fortune, the two men sailed on for several more days.

One day about this time, my father startled me by calling attention to a novel sight far in front of us, almost at the horizon. 'It is a mock sun,' exclaimed my father. 'I have read of them; it is called a reflection or mirage. It will soon pass away.' But this dull-red, false sun, as we supposed it be, did not pass away for several hours; and while we were unconscious of its emitting any rays of light, still there was not time thereafter when we could not sweep the horizon in front and locate the illumination of the so-called false sun, during a period of at least twelve hours out of every twenty-four. It could hardly be said to resemble the sun, except in its circular shape, and when not obscured by clouds or the ocean mists, it had a hazy-red, bronzed appearance which would change to a white light like a luminous cloud, as if reflecting some greater light beyond. We finally agreed in our discussion of this smoky furnace-coloured sun that, what-

ever the cause of the phenomenon, it was not a
reflection of our sun, but a planet of some sort—a
reality.

The boat's compass also indicated that something else very
strange was happening.

The compass, which we had tightly secured in its place
for fear of another storm, was still pivoting due north,
and moving on its pivot, just as it had at Stockholm.
The dipping of the needle had ceased. What could this
mean? Our many days of sailing had certainly carried
us far past the North Pole—and yet the needle continued to point north. We were sorely perplexed, for
surely our direction was now south?

During the next fifteen days, according to Olaf Jansen's
narrative, the occupants of the fishing boat saw the shore-
lines of several distinct landmasses, some flat and others
with noticeable mountain ranges. Finally, they decided to
land on one. As they wandered about, they discovered a
landscape of fast-flowing rivers, fine trees and a wealth of
flora much the same as they were used to, but all considerably larger. The 'sun' again caught their attention, as Olaf
recalled later.

In the meantime we had lost sight of the sun's rays,
but found a radiance 'within' emanating from the dull-
red sun which had already attracted our attention. It
was now giving out a white light seemingly from a
cloud-bank far away in front of us. It dispensed a
greater light, I should say, than two full moons on the
clearest night. In twelve hours this cloud of whiteness
would pass out of sight as if eclipsed, and the twelve
hours following corresponded with our night . . .

My father and I commented between ourselves on the fact that the compass still pointed north, although we now knew that we had sailed over the curve or edge of the earth's aperture, and were far along southward on the 'inside' surface of the earth's crust which, according to my father's estimate and my own, must be about three hundred miles in thickness from the 'inside' to the 'outside' surface. Relatively speaking, it is no thicker than an egg-shell, so that there is almost as much surface on the 'inside' as on the 'outside' of the Earth.

The great luminous cloud or ball of dull-red fire which we decided to name 'The Smoky God'—fiery-red in the mornings and evenings, and beautifully white at night—is seemingly suspended in the centre of the great vacuum 'within' the earth, and held to its place by the immutable law of gravitation, or a repellant atmospheric force, as the case may be. In reality it is stationary, and the effect of night and day 'within' is therefore produced by the earth's daily rotation.

According to Olaf Jansen, the extraordinary odyssey of the two men continued for 'a hundred or more days that beggared description'. At the same time subtle changes occurred in the sea and the climate through which they were sailing:

The month we reckoned to be November or December, and we sensed that the so-called South Pole was turned toward the sun. Therefore, when passing out and away from the internal light of 'The Smoky God' and its genial warmth, we would be met by the light and warmth of the Sun, shining in through the south opening of the earth. We were not mistaken.

Then, once again, the Jansens' boat was caught by surges of increasingly large waves as it was driven forward by the warm winds of the inner world. Gradually they became conscious of the air growing colder and noticed a number of icebergs on the horizon.

We were soon amid ice-packs, and how our little craft got through the narrow channels and escaped being crushed I know not. The compass behaved in the same drunken and unreliable fashion in passing over the southern curve or edge of the earth's shell as it had done on our in-bound trip at the northern entrance. It gyrated, dipped and seemed like a thing possessed.

For days the two seamen were forced to manoeuvre their little craft through the icebergs until at last open water appeared before them. But just when they appeared to be safe, the boat struck a partly submerged iceberg and both were thrown overboard. Olaf fell, unconscious, onto the iceberg. When he awoke several minutes later, there was no sign of his father. And although the young man searched frantically all around the iceberg and scanned the ocean, there was no trace of Jens Jansen or the boat.

Without food or any protective clothing, Olaf Jansen prepared himself to die bravely. Then, suddenly, a ship hove into view. Hardly daring to believe his eyes, Olaf recognised the vessel as a Scottish whaler with the name, the *Arlington*, on it side. Later he was to discover she had sailed in September from Dundee to hunt whales in the Antarctic. Waving frantically, Olaf managed to attract the attention of the boat and her crew and half an hour later was safely on board. The Captain, Angus MacPherson, proved to be a kindly, dour old seafarer, but a man not given to listening to tales of what he considered pure fantasy.

'When I attempted to tell him that I had come from

'inside' the earth, the captain and mate looked at each other, shook their heads, and insisted on my being put in a bunk under the strict surveillance of the ship's doctor,' Olaf Jansen recalled. After a period of rest and with several good meals inside him, he decided against speaking about his experiences any more. Instead he offered to work his passage home.

It was to be another year before Olaf Jansen finally reached his home in Stockholm. There he learned that while he and his father had been away, his mother had died. For a second time, the young man recounted his adventure to his only surviving relative, an uncle, Gustaf Osterlind. Since he had been picked up in the Antarctic, he had had plenty of time to reflect on his strange journey and now wanted to persuade his relative to finance an expedition to the 'inner world'.

> At first I thought he favoured my project. He seemed interested and invited me to go before certain officials and explain to them—as I had to him—the story of our travels and discoveries. Imagine my disappointment and horror when, upon the conclusion of my narrative, certain papers were signed by my uncle and, without warning, I found myself confined in a mental institution. There I was to remain for 28 long, tedious and frightful years.

In October 1862, according to Jansen's account, he was released from the institution. His uncle had died during the intervening years and he now found himself, a man over fifty, with no friends and a record of insanity. What else was there for him to do but go back to sea? For the next 27 years he worked as a fisherman, devoting his spare time to searching for evidence that his experiences in the Hollow Earth had not been just a dream. He gathered together a collection of books on polar exploration, made endless notes and drew painstaking maps. But not once during this time did he speak to another living soul about his strange voyage.

In 1889 Jansen, now well into his seventies, sold his boat and decided to move to the warmer climate of America. For twelve years he lived quietly in Illinois before moving to Glendale, Los Angeles, on 4 March, 1901, a date he remembered clearly as the day of President McKinley's second inauguration. There he settled unobtrusively in a little property, passing the time growing flowers and a few fig trees until the day he met Willis George Emerson.

Emerson (1856–1918) was a novelist and short story writer who had moved to Los Angeles in 1907 with his wife, Bonnie, to work in the embryo film industry. As a popular author of Westerns, he had sensed there would be a demand for his kind of material after the huge success of the Wild West movie *The Great Train Robbery*, released in 1903. It was a good decision, because that very year of 1907, the star of *The Great Train Robbery*, Gilbert Anderson, created 'Broncho Billy'—probably the first famous character figure in cinema history—in a two-reeler called *The Bandit Makes Good*. This was to prove the first in over 400 episodes about the cowboy hero and meant a continuous series of assignments for writers like Willis Emerson.

Although Emerson and his wife lived just a couple of blocks away from Olaf Jansen, the scriptwriter only gradually became aware of the white-haired old man as he passed him on his way to and from the studios. Jansen was often to be seen in his garden, but he mostly seemed lost in thought, Emerson was to reflect later. One spring morning, however, he gave him a cheery wave and so started a friendship that would later become a literary partnership. As Emerson wrote:

I soon discovered that my new acquaintance was no ordinary person, but one profound and learned to a remarkable degree. A man who, in the later years of his long life, had dug deeply into books and become strong in the power of meditative silence. I encouraged him to talk and in the days and weeks that followed I became well acquainted with Olaf Jansen and, little by little, he told me his story so marvellous that its very daring challenged reason and belief. The old man always expressed himself with so much earnestness and sincerity that I became enthralled by his strange narrations.

Jansen also showed Emerson his notes and maps as he recalled every detail of his voyage into the 'inner world'. Pressing them into the writer's hands he said, 'I leave them to you if I can have your promise to give them to the world. I desire that people may know the truth, for then all the mystery concerning the frozen northland will be explained.'

Despite some reservations Emerson agreed, and the result was *The Smoky God; or, A Voyage to the Inner World*, narrated by Olaf Jansen in his own words which Emerson delivered to his publishers, Forbes & Company, in Chicago. The book was published in the spring of 1908 but sadly, Olaf Jansen had died just a few weeks earlier. This time, however, he would not have to listen to any ridicule or risk being locked away.

In his foreword to *The Smoky God*, Emerson admitted that many readers would find the story hard to believe—as he himself had done. 'However much the statements in this book are at variance with the cosmographical manuscripts of the past,' he wrote, 'they may be relied upon as a record of the things Olaf Jansen claims to have seen with his own eyes. There is a saying, ancient as the hills, that "truth is stranger than fiction" and in a most startling manner has this axiom been brought home to me while writing this book.'

Emerson also noted that his informant had come to the conclusion that, as some of the old legends said, mankind had probably orginated in the Hollow Earth and it was there the fabled 'Garden of Eden' had once existed. The legend of Noah and the Ark was merely a distortion of the truth, claimed Jansen: a group of men and women had countless years ago sailed out from the inner world—just as he and his father had done—to colonise the surface of the planet.

Although today Olaf Jansen's place in the history of the Hollow Earth enigma is well recognised, copies of Emerson's book are very scarce indeed. An article in *Fate* magazine in March 1966, debating whether the old seaman's story was merely a delusion resulting from his shipwreck or a true account in every respect, noted, 'Whatever the answer, it still needs to be asked why were two copies of this book removed from government files?'

A number of Hollow Earth researchers have suggested there has been—may well still be—a conspiracy of silence among some governments about keeping secret material relating to the subterranean world. Is there reason to suspect that *The Smoky God* could be among these items?

In the decade before his own death, Willis Emerson admitted to being sceptical about certain parts of Olaf Jansen's story. He had, however, found evidence in the writings of a number of earlier polar explorers which confirmed several of the phenomena reported by the old seaman. What he *never* doubted was his neighbour's sincerity. In his foreword to *The Smoky God* he concluded:

If it was madness, then it was an eloquent madness that so appealed to my imagination that all thought of an analytical criticism was effectively dispelled. A hundred times I have asked myself whether it is possible that the world's geography is incomplete and the startling narrative of Olaf Jansen is predicated upon demonstrable facts. The reader must answer these queries to his own satisfaction.

*   *   *

Whatever controversy it may have stirred up, Olaf Jansen's narrative encouraged further examination of the Hollow Earth legend. Indeed, during that same period around the turn of the century, several more studies of the theory were published, two of which are especially important to our story.

The Phantom of the Poles by William Reed appeared in 1906 and is something of a landmark in being the first compilation of scientific evidence based on the reports of polar explorers in support of the theory that the Earth is hollow and has openings at its poles. Reed was a geography graduate of New York University, who worked for a shipping line in the city. He had become interested in the whole concept after reading an article about Symmes' Concentric Spheres. He concluded that the former soldier was on the wrong track and turned to the records of the various explorers who had visited the poles and provided accounts of their experiences, in order to try to find an alternative explanation.

Among the men whose papers and books Reed studied were Sir John Franklin (1786–1847), the British explorer who led two expeditions into the Arctic regions to find the Northwest passage, the second of which, in 1845, resulted in the loss of the entire company of 129 men. He also found much of interest in the accounts of the American Elisha Kane (1820–57) who went seeking the lost Franklin party and gave his name to the Kane Basin; the reports of George Wallace Melville (1814–1912), a US naval engineer who led the ill-fated De Long expedition in 1879; and the papers of Adolphus Greeley (1844–1935), a former American army officer who had commanded an expedition to establish a chain of meteorological stations in the Arctic. But perhaps the most important clues of all that Reed found were in the documents of the Norwegian explorer Fridtjof Nansen (1861–1930), who provided so much valuable information about the Arctic environment, and Robert Peary (1856–1920), the Pennsylvania-born explorer whose equally determined efforts to reach the North Pole were described in his book *Northward* (1902).

Reed went through all the information provided by these resourceful explorers with a scholar's eye before publishing his detailed 288-page book which, like *The Smoky God*, is now difficult to find. In it he declared: 'The earth is hollow. The Poles, so long sought, are phantoms. There are openings at the northern and southern extremities. In the interior are vast continents, oceans, mountains and rivers. Vegetable and animal life are evident in this New World, and it is probably peopled by races unknown to dwellers on the Earth's surface.'

According to the facts he had sifted, William Reed felt confident in declaring:

That the earth is hollow is proved by the fact that no one can get to the poles. In recent years all explorers have made practically the same progress—for 80 to 84 degrees of latitude—and all agree that they find it warmer and with an open sea. The difference of a few degrees is owing to the longitude as well as the latitude when taking observations. The land is not necessarily the farthest north. The curve leading to the interior of the earth may be land or water, just as it happens, and he that passes to the farthest point of the circle when the observation is taken, will show the farthest point north. But if he continues straight on he will soon be losing ground, or getting farther from the supposed pole, and eventually be going south and not know it, as the compass could not then be depended upon.

Reed estimated that the Earth started to curve in at 70 to 75 degrees north and south latitudes, and the poles were actually the outer rim of a magnetic circle around the polar openings. This meant that the poles, as we understood the term, were really in *mid-air*. It would be impossible for any explorer to claim to have reached one or other of the poles as he would be misled by the eccentric behaviour of the compass. For in either the north or south latitudes the needle would point vertically down, a phenomenon which the author noted many polar explorers had experienced.

Reed concluded his book with these words:

I have quoted from nearly all the explorers ... and their remarks prove beyond doubt that what I claim is true—that the Arctic and Antarctic oceans are bodies of open water, abounding with game of all kinds, and much warmer than farther inland. If that is true, then why have the poles not been reached? The poles are but phantoms—the earth is hollow, or all principle of reasoning must fail!

The second book, *A Journey to the Earth's Interior; or, Have the Poles Really Been Discovered?* by Marshall B. Gardner, appeared seven years later, in 1913. It was published by the author himself in his home town of Aurora, in Kane County, Illinois, and like Reed's books is hard to find today. Curiously, Gardner makes no mention of *The Phantom of the Poles* in his text or bibliography, so there is no way of knowing whether or not he had read the book. He does, however, refer to Symmes and another Hollow

Earth champion called 'the prophet Koresh' (of whom more later) in making his claim that the earth is hollow with polar openings. Where he differed from his predecessors was in his belief that there had to be a central sun in the middle of the inner earth.

Gardner, a factory worker in Aurora, was a dedicated student of the Hollow Earth legend. He claimed to have devoted almost a quarter of a century to writing his 456-page book which was packed with photographs from the Arctic and Antarctic regions, as well as numerous diagrams. The most crucial of these to his theory is reproduced here:

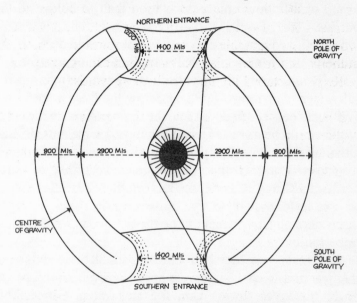

Diagram by Marshall B. Gardner of the Hollow Earth, as published in his book *A Journey to the Earth's Interior*

According to Gardner, the earth has circular openings at the poles through which the ocean waters flow. Water is able to adhere to the solid crust both above and below the hole because the centre of gravity resides in the middle of this crust and not in its hollow interior. If a ship were to travel through a polar opening and reach the interior, said Gardner, it would continue to sail in a reversed position on the inside of the crust, held to it by gravity. He was also convinced that the gravitational pull around the curve from the exterior to the interior of the earth would have a marked effect on any explorer. A 150-pound man, say, would probably weigh 300 pounds as he sailed through the polar opening, but when he reached the inside he would weigh only 75 pounds. Gardner's explanation for this was that less gravitational force would be required to hold a body to the *inside* of a hollow object in rotation than to hold it to the outside.

He believed that this gravitational pull would be so strong at the polar openings that halfway round the curve the salt water would mix with the fresh water from the interior; the salt water remaining a few feet below the fresh water. Like William Reed, Gardner felt that the temperatures in the inner world would be more uniform than those on the outside; that although there was plenty of rain, it was never cold enough for snow. A perfect subtropical climate, according to Gardner, and a 'Land of Paradise' just waiting to be claimed by anyone bold enough to try. In his closing pages he urged the American Government to be the first to 'grasp this great opportunity'.

So certain was Marshall Gardner about his conclusions that just prior to publishing the book he applied for a patent on his discovery to the United States Patent Office. This was filed on 25 November, 1912, and granted US Patent Number 1096102 on 12 May, 1914. The existence of this document has remained to this day a little-known secret outside the ranks of a few dedicated researchers, while at the same time being one of enormous significance *if* it is proven.

Taking a lead from Symmes, Marshall Gardner also sent copies of his book to a number of distinguished US Congressmmen and to several heads of state in Europe. The evidence suggests that the work was acknowledged by most recipients, although very few offered any comment. One exception was Sir Arthur Conan Doyle in England, already world-famous for the creation of Sherlock Holmes and becoming increasingly interested in spiritualism, who wrote to the author, 'I read your little book (and big theory) with great interest. It is so very original and actually explains so many facts, that if it were not that both poles had actually been attained, I should be a convert. But I thank you none the less for a most interesting exposition.'

Gardner, although undoubtedly delighted to receive a response, replied that the poles had actually *not* been attained—as Conan Doyle would find if he cared to read again that section of the book devoted to the unreliable performance of compasses when used near the poles.

Several reviews in American newspapers dismissed the book as 'merely a rehash of the Symmes theory'—a charge which Gardner promptly denied as 'absurd' because there was no similarity between his predecessor's idea of a series of concentric spheres inside the earth and his own theory of an open environment warmed by a central sun:

It will be noticed that Symmes has no coherent theory, or at least no observed facts, which will clearly show how the spaces between the verges of the concentric spheres are lighted and warmed. This is perhaps the point where the theory breaks down most disastrously. We have shown that there is more heat in the interior of the earth than there is outside of that realm, not less. And we have shown it from observed facts—Symmes depends on theory and he is wrong.

Gardner is also less than flattering about the work of a man he refers to as 'the mystical Koresh'. He dismisses this man's theory of a radically different hollow earth as 'purely speculative' and does not offer his readers even a quotation from 'Koresh's' writings or any information about where they might be found. In fact Koresh is another key figure in this field, who proposed not only that the earth was hollow, but that humans actually lived *inside* the planet, and he conducted a series of scientific experiments to prove it. It is his story and its ramifications that we come to next.

Five

THE PROPHET
OF CELLULAR
COSMOGONY

The Florida gulf coast, which sweeps in a great arc from Pensacola in the west to the Everglades and Florida Keys in the east, is famous for its beautiful beaches and wildlife refuges. Although the growth of Miami and the creation of Disney World on the Atlantic seaboard have turned the state into an international tourist mecca, along the shore facing the Gulf of Mexico there are still stretches of unspoiled land that have staved off the blight of mass development— places close to the Everglades, for instance, like the Corkscrew Swamp Sanctuary, Bonita Springs, the Carl E. Johnson County Park and Estero Island; all within twenty miles of bustling Fort Myers. But there is something far more unusual to be discovered here. Just over a century ago, one of the strangest Hollow Earth experiments on record took place near the town of Estero, the evidence for which still exists although it is largely ignored by local people.

Estero, which is located in Lee County, is a town of a few hundred people living unremarkable lives and occupied in growing vegetables, citrus fruit and bamboo. The place is rarely mentioned in popular gazetteers and, if at all, as 'a religious community founded in 1894'. This euphemistic remark disguises a truly extraordinary story.

In the summer of 1897, any casual visitor to this stretch of wooded coastline, with its miles of silver sand, might have been rather startled by the activities of a small group of men on the beach. All heavily bearded and dressed identically in simple linen overalls, they were busy trailing a long line of wire out into the gently lapping waters of the ocean. At first glance they might have been mistaken for fishermen; but there was no sign of any rods, and the only piece of equipment to be seen resembled a series of T-squares. They seemed to be attempting to erect a straight line with the wire running in a southerly direction, but if they were architects or geographers, or perhaps even marine biologists, what on earth was their purpose?

At the centre of the group stood a small, rather commanding figure—a clean-shaven man with restless brown eyes that were said by those who knew him to 'burn like live coals' whenever he grew enthusiastic about something. Unlike the rest he was dressed somewhat inappropriately for the beach in a Prince Albert coat and wide-brimmed black felt hat. A white silk bow tie knotted round his neck was blowing in the wind as he supervised the operation. The man's name was Cyrus Reed Tweed and with the others—all followers of his curious organisation—he was attempting to prove that human beings live not on the exterior of the world but *inside*.

Ever since Tweed had come across the theories of John Cleves Symmes, he had been attempting, literally, to turn them inside out. He was convinced that although the Earth *appeared* to be convex, this was actually an optical illusion, and that if a straight line could be extended horizontally far enough it would eventually run straight into the world's upward curve. This was the burning conviction which had brought him to the Gulf Coast beach in July 1897, armed with the strange piece of equipment made from three double T-squares which he called a 'rectilineator'. By running it along the coast for several miles he hoped, at last, to confirm thirty years of researching and promoting his idea.

From the days of his youth Cyrus Tweed had been someone looking for a cause with all the zeal of a religious fanatic. Born in 1839 on a farm in Delaware County, New York State, he was raised as a devout Baptist by his parents, Jesse and Mary Tweed. (When, later in his life, Cyrus Tweed became convinced that he *was* a prophet, he would draw attention to his father's name and the significance of a text from the Bible: 'And there shall come forth a rod out of the stem of Jesse, and a branch shall grow out of his roots.') Both parents hoped he would one day become a minister of the Church.

Instead, however, the young man was drawn into the Civil War and served as a private in the Union Army. For much of this time he was attached to a field hospital and there—like Symmes before him—began in his spare time to develop an interest in alternative science and medicine. So keen did he become on these subjects that at the end of the war he enrolled at the New York Eclectic Medical College in Utica, a centre for the then-popular medical cult of Eclecticism which studied herbal remedies. After three years at the college, Tweed graduated and a month later set himself up in Utica as a practising physician.

Again like Symmes, Tweed found himself puzzled by much that conventional science taught about the Earth. The concept of a world spinning in infinite space disturbed him as it seemed quite out of keeping with the words of the Bible in which he placed such implicit faith. He began to look for answers by practising what he called 'alchemy'—not the unorthodox chemistry of the ancient alchemists but a kind of meditation on the nature of the universe. At thirty years of age this meditation was to result in an event—a 'vision', he called it—which changed his life.

One night in 1869, as he sat alone at midnight in his

'organo-alchemical laboratory' (his study in Utica), Tweed was suddenly aware of a beautiful, ethereal woman standing in the room. After a moment of silence, the figure addressed him as the 'prophet Koresh', the Hebrew equivalent of Cyrus. She was, he knew at once, a spirit from God.

In an explanatory pamphlet he later wrote, entitled *The Illumination of Koresh: Marvellous Experience of the Great Alchemist at Utica, N.Y.*, Tweed described their subsequent conversation. The spirit told him he had lived several previous 'lives' and was now destined to become the new messiah. To fulfil his mission he must possess universal wisdom, she said, and the most vital element of this was an understanding of the Earth. According to the true cosmogony, 'the surface upon which humanity dwells is diametrically the obverse of modern scientific claims that the earth is convex.' The Bible itself confirmed this in the verse that God 'hath measured the waters in the hollow of his hand.' Tweed was to spread the word to all mankind, the spirit added before disappearing.

This 'special revelation', as Tweed later referred to it, was what he had been waiting for all his life. He at once threw himself into more research and contemplation and in 1870 published a second treatise in which he outlined the new astronomical 'facts' he had discovered and gave them a name, *The Cellular Cosmogony: The Earth a Concave Sphere*. It was issued bearing the pseudonym 'Prophet Koresh.'*

---

* There is no connection with David Koresh (alias Vernon Howell), the leader of the Branch Davidian Cult, a renegade offshoot of the Seventh Day Adventists, who believed the world was coming to an end and, in the spring of 1993, held a 51-day seige against police and federal agents at Waco, Texas. Koresh, who claimed to be the Christ, died with 85 of his members when he ordered the compound to be turned into a blazing inferno in a mass suicide on 19 April, 1993.

In the book Tweed explained that the earth was just like an egg. Mankind lived on the inside of a shell which was 100 miles thick and consisted of 17 layers. The inner five of these were made up of geological strata, on top of which lay five mineral layers, while the farthermost seven were all metallic. It was impossible to see across from one side of the shell to the other because the atmosphere was so dense, which was the reason why landmasses we knew to be on the opposite side of the world, such as Australia, could not be seen by looking upwards. This atmosphere also made it impossible to see the real sun. Instead the hollow earth was illuminated by a sort of ersatz sun which was a reflection of the original. When the real sun had its dark side towards us, said Tweed, this created the illusion of a rising and setting body which brought the night-time. The moon, too, was just a reflection, though of the Earth, and the planets were merely a host of floating 'mercurial discs'. In other words, they were not material objects at all, but focal points of light. The quandary about infinity which had puzzled Tweed for so long he now confidently explained by the 'fact' that there was actually *nothing whatsoever* outside the hollow earth.

In later chapters of *The Cellular Cosmogony* the author went into more detail about the composition of the so-called heavenly bodies, although his love of elaborate prose and pseudoscientific terms made it difficult for readers to follow many of his arguments. Planets, for instance, he described as 'spheres of substance aggregated through the impact of afferent and efferent fluxions of essence', while comets were 'composed of a cruosic force caused by the condensation of substance through the dissipation of the colouric substance at the opening of the electro-magnetic circuits, which closes the conduits of solar and lunar energy'.

Perhaps not surprisingly, the hostile reception to Tweed's book led to him being branded as a crank in some quarters and even a madman in others. But he was not a man easily deterred, replying to one particularly vitriolic review with all the assurance of one already living the role of a prophet: 'The opposition to my work is as unreasonable, absurd and idiotic as that manifested against the work of Harvey and Galileo.' Curiously, he drew no comparisons with John Cleves Symmes.

As time went by Tweed steadily drew together a small band of followers. However, as his enthusiasm for cellular cosmogony grew ever stronger, so his medical practice in Utica suffered, especially when local gossip labelled him as the 'crazy doctor'. In despair, his wife Edith left him, taking their only child, Douglas.

Not to be deflected from what he saw as his mission, Cyrus Tweed abandoned medicine and decided to tour the nation lecturing about the true nature of the Earth. Contemporary reports indicate that he was a mesmerising speaker, with a charisma that was particularly attractive to women. By the year 1886 he had several hundred followers—predominantly female—and had chosen Chicago to be his headquarters. Here, in Cottage Grove Avenue, he opened the Koreshan Unity, a small communal society where he lectured daily on his discoveries. As his following grew, posters began to appear around Chicago declaring 'We Live Inside!', explaining Tweed's philosophy. In 1894 an article in the *Chicago Herald* estimated that Tweed had probably gathered as many as 4,000 followers and raised over $60,000 from his speaking engagements. The idea of a hollow world might be bizarre, but it was not lacking in support.

Cyrus Tweed used some of this money to launch a magazine, *The Flaming Sword*, and an early leader signed 'Cyrus the Messenger' (none other than the great leader himself) clearly set the tone of the publication:

We have devoted much energy and effort to bring the question of Koreshan Universology permanently before the people for public discussion. In this effort we have been held up to insolent ridicule and most bitter persecution with the invariable rule to which every innovation upon prevailing public sentiment is subject. We have pushed our claims to a knowledge of cosmology until the advocates of the spurious 'sciences' begin to feel their insecurity.

History does not record whether Tweed in time began to feel a sense of insecurity about continuing his 'mission' in Chicago, but in 1894 he decided to move himself and his followers to a more peaceful location on the Florida gulf coast. Here, just 16 miles south of Fort Myers, he purchased a piece of land and announced the establishment of a new community to be called Estero, where he would continue his work to prove that humanity lived on the inside of the Earth. The town would in time, he said, be the 'New Jerusalem' and, ultimately, the capital of the world as he believed it to be, home to eight million believers.

In fact less than two hundred people settled in the neighbourhood, despite its idyllic climate and the beautiful scenery all around. A hand-picked group was chosen by the prophet to assist him in his work, and it was these 'scientists' who in July 1897 conducted the experiment to 'prove' the world was round on the shore opposite what is today the seven-mile-long bathing beach of Estero Island. Using the 'rectilineator', the wire was extended for four miles in the direction of the Florida Keys until it plunged into the sea.

Tweed was delighted. The line dropping beneath the water was proof to him that the earth was indeed curved like a giant egg. A subsequent report in the *Fort Myers Journal*, whose editor had been keeping a close and cynical eye on the Koresh community, stated that the only thing the experiment had proved was that the 'rectilineator' was useless. The prophet responded in typical fashion.

'To know of the earth's concavity,' he wrote in *The Flaming Sword*, 'is to know God. While to believe in the earth's convexity is to deny Him and all His works. All that is opposed to Koreshanity is antichrist.'

Despite the abuse that was heaped upon Tweed and his ideas, the community at Koresh continued to survive. *The Flaming Sword* went on carrying the message of cellular cosmogony to the world, while the prophet busied himself with two more books. One was a work of speculative fiction about the future entitled, *The Great Red Dragon: or, The Flaming Devil of the Orient*, which was not published until 1909 under another curious pen-name, 'Lord Chester', while the second, *The Immortal Manhood*, was to have embarrassing implications for Tweed.

Almost from the day Tweed and his followers had settled at Estero, they had received regular visits from the Marshal of Fort Myers, a somewhat belligerent man named Jordan, who clearly had no time for the people or their 'half-baked' ideas. He apparently harassed the women and often got into an argument with Tweed who was some two feet shorter than the law officer. On one occasion, after yet another spat, Jordan physically assaulted the leader, injuring him quite badly. With hindsight, it seems clear that these injuries hastened Cyrus Tweed's death.

Although Tweed remained totally convinced of his reasoning about the Earth until the day of his death in December 1908, he rather overstepped his credibility in the pages of his final work, *The Immortal Manhood*. For in this book he declared that after he died he would, like Christ, rise from the dead and take his followers to heaven. In due course, when the prophet breathed his last just three days before Christmas, a prayer vigil was begun over his body which continued into the new year. However, when no 'resurrection' occurred and news of Tweed's death reached the ear of the Lee County health officer who had jurisdiction over Estero, he arrived to find a rapidly decaying body. He ordered burial to take place immediately.

For Tweed's last resting-place the faithful chose Estero Island just off the coast. On this picturesque strand of trees and sand, the body was placed in a concrete tomb to ensure that it would not be desecrated by any enemies of Koreshanity. In the ensuing years the mausoleum was carefully tended by the surviving members of the community with the same dedication that they showed in continuing to publish *The Flaming Sword.* (Curiously, however, no mention of the founder's death was ever published in this journal.) Then, in the winter of 1921, a tropical hurricane struck the Florida coast, ripped across the island accompanied by huge waves, and shattered the tomb. The following morning, when the storm had abated, two members of the community found not a trace of the last resting-place of Cyrus Reed Tweed, nor any sign of his body.

It is still possible today to walk along Estero Bay and imagine Tweed and his followers carrying out their strange experiments. There are still older people living in the vicinity who remember the cult and the dwindling number of members who went on producing *The Flaming Sword* until 1949, when a fire at the magazine's printing plant brought its run to an end. Throughout this time the ideas of the founder were still being proclaimed as earnestly as ever, and in 1946 an entire issue was devoted to explaining how the prophet's alchemical views had actually forecast the dropping of the first atomic bombs on Hiroshima and Nagasaki in the closing days of the Second World War. After 1949, however, all was silence.

Surprisingly, the theory of cellular cosmogony, attracted the interest of a number of people outside America. Notable among these was a German engineer named Gustav Mengering, of Magdeburg, who embraced Tweed's ideas and in 1933 tried to repeat the experiment of bouncing an object off the side of the earth's hollow curve. He, however, used a *rocket*.

Rocket technology was still very much in its infancy at this time, although men had been dreaming about journeying into space for many years. Jules Verne for one had proposed the idea of a 'space gun' in his novel *From the Earth to the Moon* in 1865, but it was a Russian schoolteacher, Konstantin Tsiolkovsky (1857–1935), who had been the first to suggest a practical form of rocket propulsion. His far-sighted ideas—which were published at the same time as the two American brothers Orville and Wilbert Wright were making their first tentative flights at Kitty Hawk— even drew a little on the Hollow Earth concept. For in one set of plans Tsiolkovsky outlined a spacecraft, circular in shape, in which the crew members floated around inside—a remarkably accurate anticipation of weightlessness in space.

In the 1920s, experiments with liquid-fuel rockets were begun in America by Robert Hutchings Goddard and almost simultaneously in Germany by a group including a certain Wernher von Braun, who established a trial ground known aptly as the *Raketenflugplatz* or Rocket Field. (Later, of course, von Braun and a number of his colleagues would be responsible for developing the V2 rocket bombs flown against Britain in 1945 and then, after the end of the war when they all moved to America, the scientific rockets which would take men into space and a landing on the Moon.)

When Gustav Mengering learned about the experiments being conducted at the Rocket Field he decided that this offered an ideal method for proving the theory of Cyrus Tweed which had so obsessed him for the past decade. As a leading engineer in Magdeburg and a member of the City

Council, he was a person of some influence. He used this to persuade his fellow councillors that if they tested the American's concept of a Hollow Earth and it was shown to be *true*, the town would become famous all over the world. What he proposed to ask the rocket experimenters in Berlin to do was to fire a rocket vertically upwards. If it landed in Australia then Tweed had been right all along. Mengering was clearly a persuasive man, because in the winter of 1932 he set off for Berlin with the promise of financial support from the City Council. There he met Rudolf Nebel, one of the leaders of the German Society for Space Research, and outlined his scheme.

Nebel, who would later work on rocket research for the Nazi Party, was not one to pass up an opportunity like this one. He quickly drew up a financial plan for constructing a suitable rocket and scheduled a programme of launches. Accounts of the subsequent tests are rather sketchy, but there is no doubt that Nebel and his team spent many thousands of the marks provided by Magdeburg City Council in attempting to create a rocket far more powerful than any previously launched, in order to cross the great divide of Tweed's version of the Hollow Earth.

Records indicate that the first rocket trial was made in March 1933 and ended with the projectile exploding on the launching ramp. Several more explosions followed before another firing took place on 9 June. This rocket did lift off, but got no farther than the top of the ramp. A second launch on 13 June reached a peak altitude of six feet before toppling over. On 29 June, with the funds from Magdeburg exhausted and a statement from the council that no more would be forthcoming, Mengering watched anxiously as a third rocket was fired.

Everyone held their breath as the rocket ignited and slowly began to clear the launching ramp. For several seconds it really seemed as if this one would power up into the blue skies and settle the theory of cellular cosmogony once and for all. But instead, agonisingly slowly, the rocket swung from the vertical to the horizontal and flew for approximately a thousand feet before exploding into the ground. By good fortune, it had flown in the opposite direction from where Mengering and the technicians were standing.

Out of money and having exhausted the council's patience, Mengering had to abandon the project. And because of its disastrous conclusion, this might well have been the end for this particular Hollow Earth theory. In fact, the whole idea was to rise from the debris of the Rocket Field with the coming to power in Germany of Adolf Hitler. Indeed, the concept was to be utilised again in such a way that it might possibly have changed the entire course of the Second World War . . .

Six

HITLER AND THE 'PHANTOM UNIVERSE'

One morning early in March 1942, a former German fighter pilot, Peter Bender, who had served in the Imperial Air Force during World War One, was ushered into the presence of the man then busily engaged in conducting the second global conflict by which he intended to revenge the nation's earlier humiliation. Although at that moment Adolf Hitler, the Führer of Nazi Germany, was rather preoccupied with the efforts of his troops fighting the Russians in the east, he had given orders for Bender to be brought to his headquarters at Rastenburg to explain a theory that had already earned the approval of several leading members of the German Navy and, more crucially, that of the second most important man in the nation, Reichsmarschall Hermann Goering. A copy of this theory, *Die Hohl Welt Lehre*, lay open on Hitler's desk as Bender approached, threw up a salute to the seated man he had admired for many years, and waited to begin one of the most curious meetings of an era which is still notorious for the number of bizarre theories and weird pseudoscience that earned widespread currency among the hierarchy of the Third Reich.

There was something rather apt about a man explaining a Hollow Earth theory at Rastenburg, Hitler's strongly fortified encampment in an East Prussian wood, close to what is now the town of Ketzryn in Poland. Officially known as the *Führerhauptquartier Wolfsschanze*—Leader's Head-quarters Fort Wolf—the fortress had been erected by the Führer's engineers and builders in 1940–1 with special attention to a number of elements of mythology and the occult. Nearby had stood one of the great strongholds of the Teutonic Knights, and in the grounds was a civilian graveyard and the site of a holy well associated with ancient magical powers. More significantly still, Fort Wolf was aligned according to the principles of geomancy and stood at the heart of a configuration of ley lines that pointed directly towards Moscow in the northeast. A group of the Führer's advisers, steeped in the occult, had explained to him how people in ancient times used just such a configur-ation to direct psychic attacks at their enemies. Even the name Rastenburg, they said, was associated with ley lines, which made it an ideal centre of power.

Hitler had needed no further convincing about the suit-ability of the site, despite its rather gloomy aspect and the swampy woodlands all around. He ordered the building of what would become, after the Berlin Bunker, the most important of his headquarters. Yet for all this care and atten-tion to esoteric detail, the *Wolfsschanze* was still destined to be the place where the bomb plot against his life was carried out in July 1944.

There were no such forebodings in the air that March morning as Hitler worked on his various plans for a new Europe. The invasion of the Soviet Union, which he had launched the previous June, was stirring again after a horren-dous winter. For several months the advance had gone so well, taking his troops to within eighty miles of Moscow, but the arrival of snow in early October had rapidly been followed by sub-zero temperatures that had caused the Ger-man forces to grind to a halt. Unprepared though they were for such arctic conditions in terms of winter clothing and freeze-free armaments, they had held out against a counteroffensive by the Red Army and prayed for the arrival of Spring and a rapid thaw. Although their leader did not yet know it, by the Spring of 1942 the German forces had suffered 1,168,000 casualties and the tide of the war was about to begin turning inexorably against him.

Adolf Hitler's interest in the occult is, of course, well known, as is the fact that his dream of a Thousand-Year Reich was based on ancient Germanic lore about a 'super' race endowed with talismanic powers, who would one day rule the world. He had been born in the Austrian frontier town of Braunau, famous for its mediums, among them the brothers Willi and Rudi Schneider who possessed psychokinetic powers that enabled them to move objects at a distance. According to Louis Pauwels and Jacques Bergier in *The Morning of the Magicians* (1960), Hitler shared the same wet-nurse as Willi Schneider, and the two authors wondered—not altogether seriously, it must be said—whether both might have imbibed some mysterious powers in their milk! A few historians of the occult have also pondered whether the man who was later to become the leader of Germany might have had some precognitive ability. There is no doubt, however, that he believed implicitly in astrology and consulted his horoscope before making any major or political decision. Even before the war had begun this interest was public knowledge, as an article in the *Gazette de Lausanne* of 5 April, 1939, indicates.

'Nobody believes in astrology more than Herr Hitler,' the paper reported. 'Every month he asks for new astrological documents. It is not by accident that his coups are all made in the month of March. Before striking, he chooses the most favourable time indicated by the stars. And March is assuredly his best month . . .'

If Peter Bender had wanted an ideal time at which to expound to Hitler his lifelong conviction about the Hollow Earth and how it might be used to the advantage of the

German war effort, he could hardly have wished for a more propitious one. Not much more than a month before, on 25 January, 1942, Hitler had been talking about myths and legends during the course of his evening meal, as is recorded by François Genoud in *Hitler's Table Talk* (1953): 'Nothing prevents us from supposing that mythology is a reflection of things that *have* existed and of which humanity has retained a vague memory,' the Fuhrer told his companions. 'Who knows what discoveries would be made if we could explore the lands that are now covered by water?'

This, then, was the attitude of mind of the man to whom Bender poured out the ideas which he had first come across during World War One and had worked tirelessly ever since to substantiate.

Not a great deal is known about the early life of Peter Bender. He was born in Berlin, attended the city's university where he studied geography and languages, and in his mid-twenties joined the Imperial Air Force where he trained to be a pilot. On the outbreak of the First World War, he was assigned to a wing known as the 'Death Squadron', commanded by a brilliant young pilot named Hermann Goering. Despite their very different natures, the two men soon became close friends. They flew missions together over France and both were credited with a considerable number of 'kills'. From then on, however, Goering's career was to be one of unalloyed success which found him, at the end of hostilities in November 1918, as Germany's most famous living fighter pilot. Later he became a stunt pilot for a Swedish aircraft manufacturer, married a Swedish aristocrat, Emmy Sonnemann, and back in Germany joined the embryo Nazi Party in which he rapidly rose to prominence and power on the coat-tails of its leader, Adolf Hitler. In June 1941 Goering's triumphant progress was crowned when he was named by the Führer as his successor.

Peter Bender fared rather less well. In the summer of

1916, while patroling over France—and for once not in the company of his friend Goering—he was shot down by a French fighter, badly injured in the crash, and spent the next two years as a prisoner of war. Bender was not, apparently, a man driven by heroic thoughts of escape; he settled for a life of indolence in the camp while he slowly recovered his health. He did, however, enjoy reading and seized on anything related to his interest in geography. Because he could read English, his choice of material was more eclectic than most other POWs', and one day, amongst the piles of books and magazines, he came across several copies of Cyrus Tweed's *The Flaming Sword*. He was immediately fascinated by the concept of the human race living *inside* a hollow earth rather than outside, and pored over every word. His mind was still wrestling with the idea when the Armistice made him a free man again, just before Christmas 1918.

Back in Berlin, Bender met up again with his old friend Hermann Goering, and although both sensed they were destined to follow separate paths, they vowed to keep in touch. For all the faults that have been laid at his door, Goering was undoubtedly a loyal friend and was as good as his word to his former colleague.

Due to his war wounds Bender did not find it easy getting a job, but he finally secured a modestly paid post as a civil servant. He was still very preoccupied with Tweed's ideas and in his spare time wrote a series of articles for occult magazines on his interpretation of the Hollow Earth. Later he elaborated these into several pamphlets and books, in all of which he argued for a radical rethink of the nature of the world. His was not a theory, he maintained, but a doctrine– *De Hohl Welt Lehre*.

Bender was by now convinced that the universe was actually quite *small*. Human beings, he believed, lived on the inside surface of a hollow globe much the same size as orthodox geography stated, but surrounded by solid rock stretching to infinity. The inhabitants were prevented from falling off the surface by certain solar radiations. All around was a layer of air extending upwards 45 miles and then rarifying to become a complete vacuum in the centre of the globe. In this space hung the sun—a red-hot ball of rock much smaller than science realised at just 200 miles in diameter—the moon, also smaller, and what he called the 'Phantom Universe'. This was a mass of blue-grey gases through which pinpoints of light streamed; and *they* are what we refer to as stars and are not distant planets at all. Night was caused when these gases passed in front of the sun; while the shadow of the mass on the moon produced eclipses. Such was Peter Bender's explanation for what he claimed generations of astronomers had 'pretended' to see through their telescopes.

But if this were true, Bender was asked, why was a citizen of Dresden unable to look up into the sky and see Peking? Simple, he replied. Light does not travel in straight lines as the physicists say, but in a tight curve, returning to the surface within the space of a few miles. This phenomenon in its turn gives the false impression of a horizon. Bender also maintained that different wavelengths of light travelled in different curves. Finally, *Die Hohl Welt Lehre* stated that mankind was the only intelligence in the 'Phantom Universe', living in a hollow world that did not move. People were as enclosed and protected as if in a womb.

It may seem surprising that Goering with his flamboyant vanity, lust for wealth and looted works of art—not to mention his total ruthlessness in furthering Hitler's cause which earned him the epithet of 'the evil genius of Nazism'—should have taken this theory at all seriously. But his friendship with Bender ran deep and he was, above all else, a man who never dismissed any idea in which there might *just* be a grain of truth. When Peter Bender approached the hierarchy of the German Navy and showed them how his

Hollow Earth might be of assistance to them, Goering probably felt happy enough in his complicity. In any event, his instinct for intrigue had long ago taught him that it was always best to hedge one's bets. (Subsequent research has revealed that despite Goering's cynicism about many things, he was not immune to occultism. His wife, Emmy, was a firm believer in astrology and from 1938 onwards, like Hitler, regularly consulted a clairvoyant, Dr Augustus Heerman, who gave her advice on personal matters and the course of the war, and how her husband might be affected.)

Before the Nazis came to power, the German Navy had been becalmed in the backwaters of the armed forces, restricted by the Treaty of Versailles in the number of men and ships it was allowed. Not surprisingly, after Hitler's successful negotiation of the Anglo-German Naval Treaty in 1935, the naval hierarchy became among the party's strongest supporters. For although the size of the fleet was still restricted, an almost unlimited number of men and submarines was thereafter allowed. When Hitler went further and ordered a programme of naval rearmament, their delight was redoubled—and of course they were well prepared when war broke out in 1939.

So just how did the old salts of the German Navy come to view Peter Bender's doctrine of a Hollow Earth as something of practical use to them? His argument seems to have been both persuasive and very much to the point.

He agreed with their philosophy that the hardest task facing any naval commander was knowing precisely *where* any enemy ships might be. For centuries, observation had been the only means of satisfying this requirement, and although the invention of aircraft and then the development of radar had certainly helped the problem, it had not solved it. Spotter planes could all too easily miss a ship in the vastness of the ocean, while radar was limited in the area it could scan. But, said Bender, if the range of radar could be extended in some way to thousands of miles, by aiming its antennae up towards the sky rather than the horizon, what then? If his theory of the Hollow Earth was correct, then radar waves would bounce back from the inside of the globe and generate signals on the machine's cathode ray tube, so building up a picture of exactly where any enemy vessels might be lurking.

What Bender urged the naval men to do—and repeated to Hitler during their meeting at Rastenburg—was to carry out experiments using the navy's radar to prove his idea. He suggested modelling these tests on the exercise Tweed had carried out in Florida and Mengering had failed to verify in Berlin. But what *he* had in mind, he said, would work.

History does not tell us Hitler's initial reaction to all that Peter Bender had to say. What we do know is that he gave orders for the suggested experiments to be carried out in the greatest secrecy, under the jurisdiction of the Admiralty General Staff, on the Baltic island of Rugen just over 300 miles away. By a curious twist of fate, it was a location possessing an occult significance just like that of Rastenburg.

Rugen, which is perhaps best remembered today as the place where the German V1 and V2 rockets were developed and tested, had been in antiquity a pagan sanctuary where many power-raising rituals were performed. One famous legend recounts how King Waldemar I of Denmark, fearful of the power of the islanders, led a crusade against them in 1168 and razed their temples to the ground. During its long history, the 'holy island' as it was sometimes called was occupied by the Danes, the Swedes and the French, and then finally fell into German hands after the overthrow of Napoleon in 1815.

Because of its association with antiquity and the dead heroes of the past, the Nazi Party also chose Rugen as the site for the Hitler Youth Memorial. This shrine, ostensibly raised to commemorate the death of a Hitler Youth member, Hans Mallon, in 1931, was made of rough-hewn granite rocks with a traditional thatched roof and contained inside a massive monolithic altar. Stepping into the gloomy interior, lit only by daylight which seeped in through narrow windows, was said to be like stepping back thousands of years into the days of pagan myth.

It was to this island, with its ever-present reminder of ancient mysticism, that a group of German scientists and experts on radio, radar and photography arrived just a month after Peter Bender's meeting with Hitler, to put his theory to the test. They were provided with the very latest equipment German technology could muster, especially commandeered from all over the Reich, and were led by Dr Heinz Fisher, probably the country's chief expert on infra-red light, who had been summoned from his vital war work on the country's defence system. Fisher was not a happy man, believing, as he said later, that the whole idea was that of a crank. But the order he received from a member of Hitler's staff, to put all his research into abeyance and report to Berlin 'for immediate assignment', was not one he could disobey.

On a clear, bright morning in the second week of April, Dr Fisher and his team began their tests as instructed. The still-experimental infra-red apparatus was set up near the northern coast of Rugen and projected into the sky at an angle of forty-five degrees. Fisher, who had been fully briefed on Bender's ideas, decided to keep the knowledge from the other scientists and technicians: not one of them knew why they were carrying out this extraordinary exercise. While the men worked, SS agents were posted around the area to maintain maximum secrecy; soldiers also patrolled the shoreline to guard against unexpected interference from friend or enemy.

For a totally unreal week, Fisher's team operated the

equipment twenty-four hours a day. Always, it seemed to them, they were pointing in a direction in which there seemed nothing to detect. Each day every possible adjustment was made to the radar apparatus to ensure that it was not malfunctioning, while every piece of information was carefully noted down. It all amounted to . . . nothing.

Fisher, of course, knew what the tests were *supposed* to show. If Bender was right, then the infra-red rays travelling in a straight line would 'bounce' off the hollow earth and locate anything beyond the horizon. Their target was the British Fleet which was believed to be at Scapa Flow in the Orkney Islands. It was certainly true, the scientist admitted, that if there was anything in the idea, the tests would produce signals from an eighth of the way around the globe and provide Hitler with an immense advantage for the plans he was making to launch an offensive on every front of the war. But after seven days without even a single blip being received on Rugen, Fisher halted the tests and prepared his report for the Admiralty General Staff. As he wrote, he could not wait to get off the island and return to his serious work.

The failure of the tests and what happened subsequently to the main figures in the drama remained a mystery until the end of the war. In 1946, Professor Gerard Kuiper of the Mount Palomer Observatory heard about the curious events on Rugen and after a thorough investigation wrote an article for the scientific journal *Popular Astronomy*. In this he confirmed:

High Officials in the German Admiralty and Air Force believed in the theory of a Hollow Earth. They thought this would be useful for locating the whereabouts of the British Fleet because the concave curvature of the Earth would facilitate long-distance observation by

The Earth—solid globe or hollow world with entranceways at the
North and South Poles?

Sir Edmond Halley with a sketch showing his
concept of the Hollow Earth.

Marshall B. Gardner with (above) his
idea of the north polar opening to the
planet's interior and (below) the central
sun as viewed by an explorer entering the
Hollow Earth.

Rear Admiral Richard E. Byrd whose polar explorations led him to fly into the Hollow Earth. (Below) Open water in the midst of the Antarctic photographed by Rear Admiral Byrd's navigator, Captain McKinley.

Raymond Palmer, the American magazine editor who championed the Hollow Earth theory and (below) the two ESSA-3 satellite photographs of the North Pole opening taken in 1967—one clearly revealing the hole—which he first published.

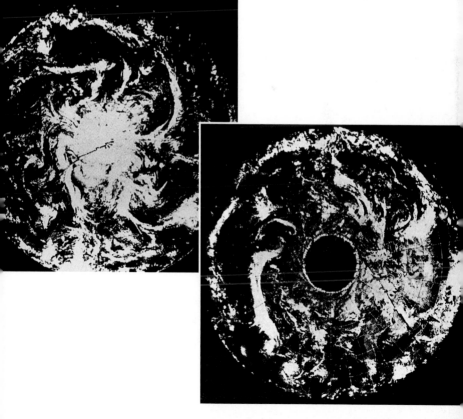

The Apollo 16 spacecraft view of the North Pole
opening taken in 1972.

Could these be the inhabitants of the Hollow Earth?
The curiously mummified figure (above) was found
in a cave deep below the Pedro Mountains in Wyoming
in 1932. (Below) A Fifties photograph of a humanoid
from a UFO of the kind believed to originate from inside
the world.

The photograph of Callisto, one of the moons of Jupiter, which
sparked the author's interest in the possibility that other worlds
might also be hollow.

John Cleves Symmes was the first man to argue that the rings of
Saturn indicated it was a hollow planet.

Two Russian scientists, Mikhail and Alexandra Chtcherbakov, have
speculated that the Moon is a hollow sphere.

Craters such as these on the surface of Mercury are believed to indicate that the planet is hollow.

One of the radar-generated photographs of Venus taken by a NASA spacecraft, which reveals a north polar opening.

American scientific researcher Ernest L. Norman believes that the interior of Mars is already inhabited by a race of peaceful aliens.

Phobos, one of the two moons of Mars, is said to be hollow as well as bearing an uncanny resemblance to an alien spacecraft in orbit.

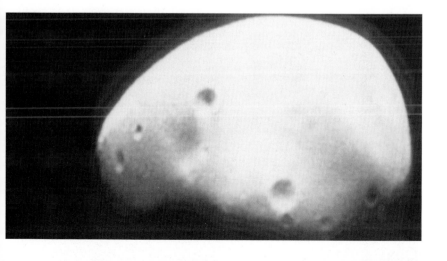

The 'Great Red Spot' on Jupiter which the Voyager I spacecraft in 1979 revealed to be a vortex which may penetrate below the planet's surface.

NASA's concept for a future world in space bears a striking similarity to the ancient idea of humanity living on the inside of a Hollow Earth!

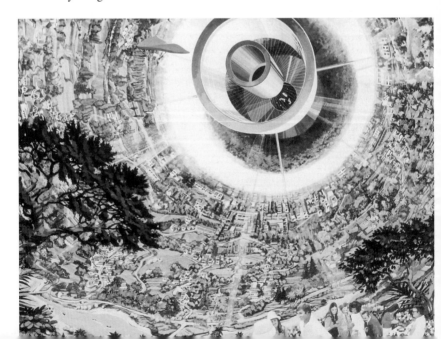

means of infra-red rays, which are less curived than visible rays.

Professor Kuiper also discovered that the man who had masterminded the tests, Dr Heinz Fisher, had survived the war and in 1945 moved to America, where he and a number of other important German scientists had been found work helping to develop the country's atomic capabilities. When confronted with the facts of his stay on Rugen, he explained simply, 'The Nazis forced me to do crazy things which hindered me considerably in my researches.'

The story does not quite end there, however. In 1957 the American Army research station at Dayton, Ohio, announced that it was developing a hydrogen bomb capable of producing a temperature of one million degrees. Among the key scientists in this astonishing programme was . . . Dr Fisher. It is chilling to contemplate, but if he had not been seconded for the Hollow Earth programme and had been allowed to continue his other researches, Hitler might have been granted an even greater prize before the Allies brought about his downfall.

The failure at Rugen cost Peter Bender dearly. Never a man to tolerate failure, Hitler ordered the proposer of *Die Hohl Welt Lehre* to be placed in a concentration camp. When Goering heard of this he knew there was nothing he could do to save his colleague. Once again Bender found himself behind bars—and this time he was not even allowed the solace of books or magazines. His last years were spent in failing health and misery amid the derision of his fellow prisoners. He died in the winter of 1944. But even on his death-bed, Peter Bender still clung to his Hollow Earth beliefs.

Nor did the theory of the 'Phantom Universe' die with him. The tests were not quite the hopeless case they were judged to be in April 1942, as Nigel Pennick has pointed out in his book *Hitler's Secret Sciences* (1981):

> The infra-red experiments on Rugen did not fail completely, for they formed the basis of a ship-detection system which the Germans tried to install across the Straits of Gibralter to monitor Allied shipping movements. Later in the war, Rugen was also used by a radar detachment tracking guided missiles launched from Pennemunde.

The name of Peter Bender survived, too. In 1948, a German admirer of *Die Hohl Welt Lehre*, Karl E. Neupart, issued a series of leaflets in which he restated what he believed to be the viability of the doctrine and affirmed the genius of its advocate. Copies of these papers still circulate today among a small group of Europeans who believe, like Bender, that the world is a globe entombed in solid rock; while Neupart's book *Geokosmos* (1953) is regarded as the most important textbook on the subject. In the Fifties, a Society for Geocosmical Research was established at Garmisch-Partenkirchen in Germany, which again adapted the theories of Tweed and his successors and published its own map of the hollow globe.

The central plank of the society's argument was that the Earth extended infinitely in all directions. There was no hidden central sun, but the familiar sun which was actually half dark and half light. It was permanently stationary, while the inside of the Earth spun around it, completing one journey every 24 hours to provide day and night. In one of its publications, the society declared in tones that would certainly have earned Tweed's approval: 'Mankind can only gain if it recognises that for good or bad it is living in an enclosed space, and at the same time is embedded in the cosmos.'

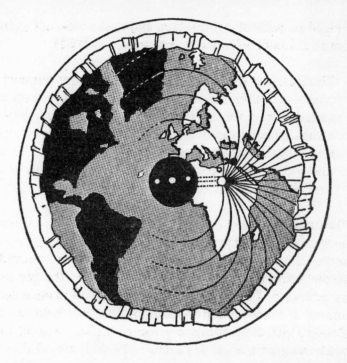

The Earth as a hollow globe, as envisaged by the German Society for
Geocosmical Research

But to return again to the Rugen experiments. Although
they effectively marked the end of Hitler's interest in the
Hollow Earth theory, he never lost his obsession with the
occult and, as history has shown, it contributed to his ulti-
mate downfall. However, stories relating to the Hollow
Earth continued to dog him and others in the Third Reich
until the end of the war. One such tale concerns a group of
Nazis who set up 'Operation Odessa', to provide an escape
route out of Germany when it became obvious that all was
lost. Among the plans of this group was one for a fleet of
submarines to take Hitler and his closest associates to a
base set up under the ice cap of the South Pole. Here they
would be safe and perhaps have time to investigate the

reports of a gateway to a subterranean world. No such romantic fate was to befall Hitler, of course, but a sordid death by his own hand in the besieged bunker in the heart of Berlin.

A curious footnote to this story takes us naturally to the next major event in the Hollow Earth enigma. In 1938, Hitler had ordered three aircraft to Antarctica, to fly over what is now Queen Maud Land. Their crews were to set up a base and then drop small swastika flags over the territory and claim it for Germany. It was to be named *Neue Schwabenland*.

With the benefit of hindsight, it seems evident that Hitler was partly interested in adding to his empire and partly in learning what lay in these regions. For years there had been speculation in Germany about 'lost cities' in the Antarctic, miraculously kept warm by volcanic activity. German archaeologists had led expeditions to the frozen continent in 1873, 1901 and 1911, and with the rise of interest in ancient myths during Hitler's era—especially that the South Pole region might once have been part of the Atlantean culture—it was ripe for additional fact-finding missions.

Unfortunately, there is no documented evidence of what actually happened to the Germans or their mission. There are claims that a secret U-boat base was established and that this continued to operate until the end of the war. But there is no proof that the men discovered anything about the legend-haunted land, although Nigel Pennick has commented significantly on this strange episode:

Perhaps this southernmost Nazi base was the final remaining outpost of the Third Reich? Several years after the fall, a military expedition under Admiral Byrd left the United States for that very territory, now claimed by Norway. Reports of US aircraft losses baldly stated, 'destroyed by enemy action' ... Byrd's now-famous flight, where he is said to have entered uncharted territory thought by some to be into the 'inner world' of the Hollow Earth, took place at this time. Perhaps he was following up Nazi research, for their interest in the Hollow Earth theory is well known. Even if he did not enter any uncharted lands, the garbled account of the Hollow Earth trip may have originated in Nazi documents seized during the expedition.

In fact, since Pennick wrote these words, a great deal more evidence has come to light, suggesting that Admiral Richard Byrd did indeed fly into the inner world. The evidence is contained in the pages of his logs and diaries, several of which have remained secret until recently. They provide a record every bit as amazing as Olaf Jansen's similar voyage by sea.

Seven

THE SECRET LOG OF
ADMIRAL BYRD

Those who met Rear Admiral Richard Byrd described him
as an archetypal all-American hero. Tall, good-looking, with
blond, curly hair, a ready smile and easy laugh, he was a
man of adventure who never shirked a challenge and always
talked about his achievements modestly, although he was
well aware of the value of publicity in promoting his aims.
As an accomplished US naval officer and pilot he was not,
however, given to flights of imagination: the elements of
sea and sky in which he spent some of the most formative
years of his life had been demanding taskmasters. He was
singleminded in all he did, inspired all those he commanded,
and was precise in describing his experiences, no matter
how unusual. As well as being a seaman and aviator, Byrd
also became a scientific explorer and is perhaps best
remembered today for his long-distance flights over the
Atlantic, his well-organised expeditions to the Antarctic,
and his survival alone for one whole winter near the South
Pole—all exploits that provided invaluable information for
subsequent pilots and explorers.

Yet this tough and resourceful man, who experienced at
first hand the climatic extremes to be found at the ends of
the earth, is another of the key figures in the Hollow Earth
enigma. For the evidence suggests that Admiral Byrd flew
into the 'inner world' via the poles on probably two

occasions, and left a record of his experiences which is every bit as astonishing as that of Olaf Jansen, though told from a quite different perspective.

Much of Richard Evelyn Byrd's life as an explorer is recounted in a matter-of-fact style in his two books *Discovery* (1935) and *Alone* (1938). Yet the story of his amazing flights in the Arctic and Antarctic, just a few years after the end of the Second World War, remains shrouded in mystery and full of unanswered questions. The log he kept of these flights is 'unavailable', despite repeated requests to the New York office of US Naval Research, and when he died in 1957 a diary he had kept of his other strange experiences when flying over the polar territories was claimed by the US Naval Intelligence Bureau in Washington and has likewise proved unavailable to scholars or the general public. But thanks to the assistance I have received from some fellow Hollow Earth researchers in Australia, I am able to present extracts from the crucial sections of both documents which have been secret for almost half a century. The contents, as you will read, are little short of amazing.

Byrd was born in Winchester, Virginia, on 25 October, 1888, and after attending the University of Virginia and the US Naval Academy, learned to fly at the Navy's Air Station at Pensacola in Florida. His early training flights were in seaplanes—the downfall of quite a number of young pilots—but he persevered and, once qualified, served with distinction during the First World War. Later, he played an important role in developing navigational aids for transatlantic crossings and began his polar career in 1924 when he commanded a small naval aviation detachment on an expedition to western Greenland. This fired him with an ambition to be the first man to fly over the North Pole, and on 9 May, 1926, he took off in a Fokker 3-engine monoplane from King's Bay, Spitzbergen. Thus he came to gaze on the area with which his name has become inextricably linked

in Hollow Earth lore. His later description of the flight in
Skywar (1928) is pregnant with inferences:

> The unknown lay ahead, we were opening up
> unexplored regions at the rate of nearly 10,000 square
> miles an hour and were experiencing the incomparable
> satisfaction of searching for a new land. Time and
> direction became topsy-turvy as we neared the Pole
> ... and here and there, instead of the pressing together
> of the ice-fields, there was a separation leaving a water-
> lead showing greenish-blue against the white of the
> snow. Once, for a moment, I mistook a distant, vague,
> low-lying cloud formation for *the mountain peaks of
> a far-away land* [my italics].

What, in fact, *did* Byrd see on that May day? The open
water was certainly a surprise, but had he also glimpsed
something beyond the pole never seen before but hinted at
from ancient times? Whatever the facts of the matter, on
his return to the United States he became a national hero,
was made a Rear Admiral and awarded a US Congregational
Medal of Honour. But some authorities felt the climax of
the flight may have been an illusion, as Richard Montague
explains in *Oceans, Poles and Airmen* (1981): 'In the early
Seventies, grave doubts were cast upon these records and,
indeed, upon Byrd's claim to have reached the pole at all.'

The first hint of a conspiracy over what the aviator had
seen? Byrd, for his part, was never in any doubt about the
curious phenomena he had witnessed and they were never
far from his thoughts on later polar expeditions.

In the autumn of 1928, after a 'warm-up' flight in June
1927 across the Atlantic from west to east, Byrd announced
that he was planning to go to the other end of the earth and
fly over the unknown regions of the Antarctic. His fame
and publicity skill enabled him to obtain financial backing

from wealthy Americans like Ford and Rockefeller, and a flood of donations poured in from the public, amounting to over $400,000. Backed by these funds, he led a large and well-equipped expedition to set up a base on the face of the Ross Ice Shelf. He named it, with a patriotic flourish, 'Little America'. Once more, the unexpected awaited Byrd when he took to the air on 29 November, 1929, as he recorded in his 1931 publication *Little America: Aerial Exploration in the Antarctic and the Flight to the South Pole*:

> It is a confusing place, this imaginary point, the South Pole. All time meridians converge there. A person unfortunate enough to be living in the vicinity would have difficult in telling just what time to keep. Directions, as we reckon them, likewise mean nothing to this unfortunate creature. For unless he was travelling either north or south, it would be impossible for him to walk in a straight line and still retain the same direction. His direction would change noticeably every few minutes; and to keep his original direction he would be forced to follow a spiral course.

As Byrd flew across the bottom of the world, strange new sensations again crowded his vision.

> Of all the flights I have made, none was so full of excitement and profit as this one. An air of impending drama foreshadowed every mile of progress. North, east, south and west—everything that was there was unseen and untrodden and unknown. Dim shapes began to loom in the southeastward, suggestive of land. They were not unlike the pyramids of Egypt in the odd looming which is characteristic of Antarctic visibility. It seemed to be very important and yet one could not exult. Nature had worked on such a large scale and

with such infinite power that one could only gape at her handiwork with open mouth and say, Holy smoke! For here was the ice age in its chill flood tide. Here was a continent throttled and overwhelmed. Here was the lifeless waste born of one of the greatest periods of refrigeration that the earth has ever known. Seeing it, one could scarcely believe that the Antarctic was once a warm and fertile climate, with its own plants and trees of respectable size.

The Rear Admiral and his navigator, Lloyd K. Grenlie, made several other flights over the Antarctic continent that winter, discovering a range of high peaks that were named Rockefeller Mountains after the expedition's benefactor and a large tract of territory which was designated Marie Byrd Land after the pilot's wife. They also, apparently, undertook a second journey in the vicinity of the South Pole, although this is not specifically mentioned in Byrd's book. The evidence of the flight is to be found in F. A. Giannini's book *World Beyond the Poles* (1959), in which he cites the evidence of a newsreel:

That year [1929] a newsreel could be seen in America's cinemas which described *both* flights. It also showed newspaper photographs of 'the land beyond the pole with its mountains, trees, rivers and a large animal identified as a mammoth'. Today this newsreel apparently does not exist, although hundreds of people remember viewing it. They *saw* things recorded on that film which proved that this unknown, uncharted and presently denied land *exists*.

Giannini maintained that Lloyd Grenlie had confirmed these facts to one of his neighbours in Nelsonville, Wisconsin, some years before his death in June 1970. The author said that the existence of the newsreel had also been confirmed to him in a number of letters from people who had seen it, including one which he quoted, from Miss Dorothy E. Graffin of New York:

Re: Admiral Byrd's flights to the South Pole and what he saw in the interior of the Earth at the South Pole. Nobody ever mentions the documentary film which Byrd took on this flight and was shown in motion picture theatres throughout the United States soon after Byrd's return home. My sister and I saw this in White Plains, New York. Byrd narrated the film himself and exclaimed in wonder as he approached a warm water lake surrounded by conifers with a large animal moving among the trees and what Byrd described as a 'mountain of coal sparkling with diamonds'.

Notwithstanding the mystery surrounding this flight, there is no doubt that Byrd returned to Little America for a second time in 1933, to explore and map new territory. Between March and August 1934, he also spent five months alone in a hut at a weather station, Bolling Advance Base, some 125 miles from Little America. Here he endured temperatures as low as −76 degrees Fahrenheit (−60 degrees Centigrade) and was finally rescued suffering from frostbite and carbon-monoxide poisoning that came perilously close to taking his life. *Alone* (1938) describes these events in harrowing detail.

Courageous as this exploit was, even weirder events awaited the intrepid adventurer after the Second World War. During the hostilities Byrd had served in the rather less demanding position of a member of the staff of the chief of naval operations. Then, in 1946, he was put in charge of a new programme named 'Operation High Jump', ostensibly to continue mapping the North and South Poles—although, as Nigel Pennick has suggested, he may also have been asked to investigate the possibility of any Nazi presence. In February 1947, before leaving for the Arctic, he again talked to the press about his plans and was quoted as saying, 'I'd like to see that land beyond the [North] Pole. That area beyond the Pole is the centre of the Great Unknown.'

According to official US sources, during his subsequent seven-hour flight across the Arctic, Byrd 'flew a distance of 1,700 miles and returned with much useful data.' Yet why is there no more specific information available about this flight which was clearly another milestone in polar exploration? And, stranger still, why did Byrd, who had set out with such high expectations of seeing 'the centre of the Great Unknown', never speak about the journey for the rest of his life?

If we accept as authentic a copy of the Rear Admiral's log which has been obtained by the Hollow Earth Society of Australia, then his wish to see the land beyond the Pole *did* come true. The document is a lengthy one which has clearly been annotated, but the extracts I have included below do seem to bear the hallmarks of Richard Byrd's style of writing and manner of expression. It is for the reader to judge whether they could be genuine or not.

Flight Log—Camp Arctic, February 19th 1947

Vast ice and snow below. Note colouration of a yellowish nature. It is dispersed in a linear pattern. Altering course for a better examination of this colour pattern below. A reddish-purple colour also. Circle this area two full turns and return to a sine compass heading. Position check made again with base. Relaying information concerning colouration in ice and snow below . . .

Both magnetic and gyro compasses beginning to gyrate and wobble. We are unable to hold our heading by instrumentation. Take bearing with sun compass but all seems well. The controls are seemingly slow to respond, have a sluggish quality. Yet there is no indication of icing . . .

In the distance is what appears to be mountains. Twenty-nine minutes of elapsed flight time and first sighting of mountains; it is no illusion. They are mountains consisting of a small range I have never seen before. Altitude change to 2950 feet . . .

Encountering strong turbulence again. We are crossing over the small mountain range still proceeding northward as best as can be ascertained. Beyond the mountain range is what appears to be a small river. A valley with a small river running through the central portion. There should be no green valley here. Something is definitely wrong and abnormal here . . .

We should be over ice and snow. From the port side there are great forests growing on the mountain side. The instruments are still spinning. The gyroscope is oscillating back and forth . . .

I alter the altitude to 1400 feet and execute a sharp left turn to better examine the valley below. It is green with either moss or a tight-knit type of grass. The light here seems different. I cannot see the sun anymore . . .

We make another left turn and spot what seems to be a large animal of some kind below. Appears to be an elephant. No, it looks more like a mammoth-like animal. This is incredible, but there it is. Decrease altitude to 1000 feet and take binoculars to better examine the animal—definitely a mammoth-like animal. Report this to base camp . . .

Encountering more rolling green hills. The external

temperature indicator reads 74 degrees Fahrenheit. Continue on our heading. Navigation instruments seem normal now. I am puzzled over their actions. Attempt to contact base camp. Radio is not functioning. The countryside is more level than normal, if I may say that word. Ahead we spot what seem like habitations. This is impossible! Aircraft seems light and oddly buoyant. The controls refuse to respond . . .

I tugged at the controls again. They will not respond. The engines of our craft have stopped running. The landing process is beginning. The downward motion is negligible and we touch down with only a slight jolt. I am making a hasty last entry in the flight log. I do not know what is going to happen now . . .

Is this a true account or merely a version attributed to Byrd? Hollow Earth researchers who have studied the log are divided. Some believe it does indeed record a journey *beyond* the Pole and in through the polar opening to the hollow earth of mountains, lakes, rivers, vegetation and life forms as legend has maintained. Others, however, are rather more suspicious of the document because of a section in it which reports that after landing Byrd met a group of tall, blond men who spoke English in 'a slightly Nordic or German accent' and greeted him with the words, 'Welcome Admiral to our domain—you are in safe hands.' After this he travelled in a strange disc-shaped machine 'with markings like a type of swastika', and was given a conducted tour of the inner world, visiting 'a glowing city which appeared to be made of crystal'. Later Byrd was allowed back to his aircraft and told to take a message to all surface dwellers about the dangers they faced if they continued to experiment with atomic weapons. To those researchers who were aware of the stories of Nazis and secret polar bases, the whole incident seemed to be rather too much of a coincidence to be true.

The document does, however, contain one further entry, for 11 March, 1947, which is much more likely to have been made by Byrd:

> I have just attended a debriefing and passed on my log. I am now detained for several hours and interviewed by the military and a medical team. It was an ordeal. I am placed under strict control of the international security provisions of the United States of America. I am ordered to remain silent in regard to all that I have seen. Incredible! I am reminded that I am a military man and that I must obey orders.

In 1955 Byrd was again 'under orders' to return to the South Pole and continue mapping the territory. Despite the restrictions which had been placed upon him, the Rear Admiral spoke to the press before sailing to the Antarctic in the aircraft carrier *Philippine Sea*, in November 1955, telling reporters, 'This is the most important expedition in the history of the world.'

Yet, once again, the official statement after the assignment was over was blunt to the point of banality: 'Rear Admiral Byrd made a second flight over the South Pole and took part in several other flights. A total of 437,000 square miles of Antarctic territory was discovered and mapped.'

This communiqué completely ignores a much more revealing radio announcement issued from Little America on 14 January, 1956 and later reprinted in many national daily newspapers in America and elsewhere: 'On January 13, members of the United States expedition accomplished a flight of 2,700 miles from the base at McMurdo Sound, which is 400 miles west of the South Pole, and penetrated a land extent of 2,300 miles beyond the pole.'

A quick look at a map of the world will immediately reveal the discrepancy in this report. The Antarctic is, of course, surrounded by water, and it is impossible to travel a distance of 2,300 miles *in any direction* without traversing water. So where could this land over two thousand miles away be but inside the Hollow Earth?

In public at least, Byrd was circumspect when he returned from the South Pole on 13 March to be greeted as 'the world's greatest explorer'. The expedition had, he said, 'opened up a vast new territory' and he spoke lyrically of 'that enchanted continent in the sky, land of everlasting mystery'.

Yet almost as quickly as the interest in Byrd's discoveries had grown, so it seemed to dissipate, with the newspapers, radio and newsreels turning to other items of news closer to home. If the Rear Admiral *had* discovered an inner world which could change forever mankind's perception of the earth, the media, it seemed, was too preoccupied to take any more notice. Or was it? Dr Raymond Bernard, in his pamphlet *The Hollow Earth* (1969), thinks the explanation is rather different:

Admiral Byrd's discovery is today a leading international top secret, and it has been so since it was first made in 1947. After Byrd made his radio announcement from his plane and after a brief press notice, all subsequent news on the subject was carefully suppressed by government agencies. The explanation is evident. If Admiral Byrd made such a momentous discovery, undoubtedly the greatest one in history, of a new unknown land area of undetermined extent, over which his expedition flew for a total of 4,000 miles at each pole, and which area is probably as wide as it is long, and, since Byrd turned back before reaching its end, is probably much larger than an area 4,000 miles square, then it would be in the interest of the US government to keep this discovery secret, so that other nations do not learn about it and claim this territory for themselves.

Victim of a conspiracy theory or not, Rear Admiral Richard Evelyn Byrd finished his career weighed down with medals and citations for his expeditions and his exemplary conduct. When he died in Boston on 11 March, 1957, the authorities honoured him as a national hero and he was buried in Arlington National Cemetery, Virginia, with full military honours. But to the grave with him went the secrets of precisely *what* he had seen while flying over the poles. A final paragraph in his diary does not answer all the questions, but certainly indicates that Byrd believed there was more to the Arctic and Antarctic wastes than just endless miles of frozen snow:

December 24, 1956. These last few years since 1947 have not been so kind. I now make my final entry in this singular diary. In closing I must state that I have faithfully kept this matter secret as directed all these years. It has been completely against my values and moral rights. Now I seem to sense a long night coming on, and this secret will not die with me, but as truth shall, it shall triumph. It is the only hope for all mankind. I have seen and it has quickened my spirit and set me free. I have done my duty towards the monstrous military industrial complex. Now the long night of the Arctic ends, the brilliant sunshine of truth shall come again, and those who are of darkness shall fail in flight. For I have seen that land beyond the poles, the centre of the great unknown.

Underneath is scrawled the familiar signature, 'Richard E. Byrd, United States Navy'.

Eight

HOLES IN THE TOP OF
THE WORLD

Among the most revealing pieces of evidence in the Hollow Earth enigma are four photographs of the North Pole, all taken from space. They show a circular opening where the polar icecap should be. Three of these were shot in 1967 and 1968 by orbiting satellites and the fourth in April 1972, apparently by Apollo 16 on its journey to the Moon. All have been the subject of considerable controversy and speculation—do they actually reveal the entranceway to the inner earth or are they just photographs of freak weather conditions? Because they may be important pieces of evidence, copies of two of the most impressive photographs appear in the plates section of this book.

The first two pictures were taken in January and November 1967 by satellite cameras. On 6 January, a circling US Environmental Science Service Administration weather satellite, ESSA-3, nearing the end of its 'tour of duty', having taken almost a million and a half photographs, produced a shot of the North Pole in which, instead of the normal mass of white clouds, a black, indistinct mass obscured the whole region. Later in the year, on 18 November, an ATS-III satellite camera with a vantage point from the Equator captured on film what seemed like a huge, dark crater where the Arctic Circle was normally to be seen. Curious as both pictures were, they excited no real interest

among the ESSA officials in Washington DC, who filed
them along with millions of other exposures. It was not
until a third and much more detailed photograph of the
Arctic region was taken that anyone began to believe something extraordinary had occurred.

This third exposure was again just one of a huge batch
of radio-received exposures, transmitted from an ESSA-7
satellite on 23 November, 1968, as it circled the world
filming the changing weather conditions. (During its 481
days in space, the ESSA-7 took a total of 39,953 pictures
before being put on 'stand-by mode', the Administration
records indicate.) The other photographs taken by the satellite all show the usual patterns of swirling clouds over the
vast land masses and oceans of the world. But this
anomaly—so it is believed—caught a moment when the
normally dense weather system over the North Pole cleared
briefly to allow the camera in the sky a view of the legendary
gateway to the Hollow Earth.

For two years this remarkable photograph went unnoticed
until it was spotted by a researcher and—thanks to the
freedom-of-information policy of ESSA—released for publication. Not surprisingly, the first appearance of the picture
in the June 1970 issue of *Flying Saucers* magazine created
a sensation. It was also something of a coup for the publication's editor, Ray Palmer, who had for years been cham-
pioning a number of controversial science subjects,
including alien intervention, UFOs and the Hollow Earth.

Palmer, who died in 1977, is still regarded as one of the
most important figures during the period of the late Forties
when interest first began to develop in what are popularly
referred to as 'Flying Saucers'. He was a man of strong
opinions, never afraid of controversy, and always willing to
defend himself feistily when accused, as he was on several
occasions, of masterminding a hoax to sell his books or
magazines. He was in many respects in the same mould as

the current wave of writers on the unexplained, such as Erich von Däniken, Charles Berlitz and Graham Hancock. Palmer's resolute stand against those who attacked him or ridiculed his beliefs was all the more commendable because of his diminutive stature and poor health.

Raymond Arthur Palmer—'Rap' to his friends—was born in Milwaukee, Wisconsin, on 1 August, 1910, and suffered a childhood plagued by accidents and illness. He broke his back in a car accident at the age of seven, fell off a roof at ten, and by the time he reached adulthood stood at just four feet eight inches tall. Confined to bed for several of his formative years, Ray found escape in the world of science fiction, filling his imagination with the novels of Jules Verne, H. G. Wells and Edgar Rice Burroughs, as well as the first magazine to cater for this growing interest, *Amazing Stories*. The ideas that all these works put into his mind left him in no doubt about where his future lay. In 1930 he published the first sf fanzine in America, *The Comet*, and soon afterwards began contributing to *Amazing Stories* and its rivals, *Astounding Stories* and *Wonder Stories*. His reputation grew rapidly and in February 1938 he was offered the job of editor of the Chicago-based magazine that had inspired his fascination, *Amazing Stories*.

It was in this editorial chair that Ray Palmer was to make his name, first by continuing to publish Edgar Rice Burroughs and, second, by printing 'Marooned off Vesta', the debut story of the legendary Isaac Asimov. More significantly, he was fascinated by the unexplained, as presented in Charles Fort's works, and he used his position to look for answers to some of the strangest cases. Believing, for instance, that Jesse James was still alive, he sent the great detective John Shevlin to track down the outlaw; and when the pilot Kenneth Arnold coined the term 'Flying Saucers' to describe some unidentified objects he saw in the sky, it was Palmer who in 1952 co-authored his ground-breaking book *The Coming of the Saucers*. (This just two years after an accidental fall had left him paralysed from the waist down in a condition that doctors had wrongly diagnosed as permanent. He turned this to his own advantage by telling a story that when people met him for the first time, they would almost invariably exclaim, 'Oh, you really *are* the man from Mars!')

Although Palmer was once very publicly accused by a US Air Force spokesman of having generated the entire UFO mystery as a publicity campaign, he was quick to point out that he did not actually believe in the popular concept of Flying Saucers. 'I really *don't* believe in them,' he told *Saga* magazine in 1965, 'at least not in the popular concept of flying saucers that the public interprets as being synonymous with alien spacecraft from outer space. I *do* believe in whatever reality is behind the flying saucer mystery—but this reality is at the present time unknown.'

In 1949 Palmer resigned as editor of *Amazing Stories* and returned to his native Wisconsin to start his own publishing house. Here, at Amherst, he converted an old school building into the headquarters of a group of magazines whose titles clearly indicate their contents: *Fate* (which continued the same line of enquiry into inexplicable phenomena that Charles Fort had instigated), *Search*, *Space World* and *Rocket World* (all dealing with the future of space travel and the possibility of alien lifeforms), and *Flying Saucers* in which he campaigned for more civilian flying saucer research and often confounded and irritated the scientific establishment with his claims. Few of these topics generated more heat than the case of the 'Hole in the Top of the World'.

Palmer was unable to accept the extraterrestrial origin of UFOs and was inclined to believe that they might come from much nearer home. In 1968 he wrote an editorial for *Flying Saucers* in which he put this belief into words:

The more we consider the extra-terrestrial thesis, the more impossible it becomes to prove. UFOs have been seen in the skies since man's prehistory, and today there seems to be a virtual traffic jam of objects coming in from somewhere. It seems to me difficult to conceive that ours should be the only planet of any interest to extra-terrestrial life forms. Therefore the supposition that the saucers have an earth base and may be manned by an older terrestrial race brings the cosmic concept down to reality. Geographically speaking, of course, our own atmosphere is a great deal closer than Alpha Centauri!

It seemed to Palmer that there might be some connection between these UFOs and the ancient legend of a Hollow Earth which he had read about in a number of publications. In another article that same year, he mentioned the way his mind was working: 'I cannot deny the possible existence of underground cultures. One can find references to them in the most primitive oral traditions and right up to contemporary accounts.'

If Raymond Palmer was hoping for further evidence to support the idea of a world beneath the surface of the Earth, he could hardly have expected anything quite like the ESSA-7 photograph which landed on his desk. Unknown to him, of course, the picture had been in existence since 1968, but it had taken a sharp-eyed UFO researcher in Washington to spot the dark, circular area at the North Pole and send a copy to Palmer. The correspondent also enclosed a comparative photograph of the polar region swathed in clouds which had been taken on the same day. The writer added that the unique picture was completely unretouched. The grid patterns of latitudes to be seen on it had been printed automatically by computer calculations when the picture was taken, he said, and formed an integral part of the photograph, enabling the Environmental Science Service officials to identify precisely the areas shown. (The area depicted is about 40 per cent of the Earth's surface and clearly shows part of the North American continent, Greenland and some of the Asian continent.)

Confirming with Washington that the photograph was genuine, Palmer wasted no time in publishing it on the front cover of the June 1970 issue of *Flying Saucers*. Inside, in an editorial, he declared his unequivocal belief in the picture:

> One of the severest criticisms levelled at us during past years because of our theorising concerning a hole at the pole and a Hollow Earth, has been the fact that none of the photos taken from satellites have shown such a hole. There have been a half-dozen taken from orbits which have shown the dark area visible in the photo, but they were impossible to record as definitive photographic resolution of such a phenomenon as a hole. *Now we have a photo!*

Palmer forestalled any accusations that it was asking too much to make such a claim, based on a single photograph which could have resulted from a defect in the camera or its lens, by specifically citing the ESSA-3 and ATS-III photographs which his researcher in Washington had also uncovered meanwhile. Underneath these two pictures which, unfortunately, did not reproduce anywhere near as well as the ESSA-7 photograph, he declared forcibly:

> If UFOs have been in the top secret file, then the place they might come from certainly *would* be! And apart from flying saucers, there are many more reasons why a hole at the pole would be classified information. Militarily, it would be highly significant—particularly

if the inside of the earth is inhabited, perhaps by a race far superior to us, scientifically and technologically!

More modern concepts of the formation of planets adopt the 'vortex' or 'whirlpool' theory. This states that bodies in space are formed by a rotating motion in the ether which collects matter at its centre, gradually adding to it until it becomes a sun or planet or a satellite or a comet. The semi-spherical object has the typical formation of a vortex, such as you observe in water going down a drain with a 'hole at the centre of a swirl'. Thus, in this theory quite widely held by astronomers and physicists, many planetary bodies still have this hole at the centre of the whirl that has formed them.

The opinions that greeted the publication of the photographs and Palmer's editorial were, as might be expected, poles apart. The cynical asked why, as several airlines advertised the fact that they flew over the North Pole every day, this so-called 'hole' had not been seen many times before. (In fact, polar flights are rarely within 150 miles of the geographic pole because of possible interference to the navigational instruments.) Other readers found it difficult to believe that the cloud cover was so constantly dense as to produce only a couple of pictures amongst all the millions taken at the time, and demanded more data. But for believers—especially men like the respected British UFO author Brinsley Le Poer Trench, the ESSA-7 shot was a major piece of evidence in the enigma of the Hollow Earth.

Le Poer Trench (1911–1995), who was actually the eighth Earl of Clancarty and Chairman of the all-party UFO Study Group in the House of Lords, had himself been investigating the possible terrestrial origins of UFOs, as his books *The Flying Saucer Story* (1966) and *Operation Earth* (1969) bear witness. Greatly excited by the ESSA photograph, he told the London newspaper *The Sunday Times* in October 1974, 'It is one of the most exciting and remarkable photographs ever taken, clearly showing the North Polar entrance which mankind has been seeking since time immemorial.'

Some writers to *Flying Saucers* were less complimentary. One correspondent claimed the photograph was a 'composite paste-up, placed over a sphere for reproduction' (which Palmer denied and ESSA confirmed was not the case), while another who said he was a radioscope operator in the Arctic region wrote that a number of government scientific specialists had travelled all over the Arctic 'without seeing any evidence of the hole'. Palmer, again, was quick to take up his pen in defence of the photograph, as well as to widen his argument:

Recently, the most fascinating discovery of the polar area has been the revelation that as we approach the pole the surface of the ocean *begins* to slant towards the north. Now every high school student knows that the absolutely infallible way to find a level and construct something on that level is to use the surface of water which *never* tilts. Now why, 800 miles from the pole, does the water suddenly begin to tilt in that direction? Obviously gravity has something to do with it. Either gravity is no longer functioning directly toward the centre of the earth, or the centre of the mass is being dislocated (by the fact of an increasing angle of descent into a depression, the surface of which is at right angles to this displacement of the centre of gravity of the Earth's mass?). Lots of strange things happen in the polar regions as explorers have described—like the distance to the east-west horizon being greater than the distance to the north-south horizon, which so baffled Nansen—and it would take a very thick book to present all the facts that are not

explainable without postulating some such thing as a
hole at the pole or a Hollow Earth.

Palmer then threw down a challenge: 'I had a very good
reason for publishing the photographs in my magazine.
There is not a person in this world who has ever read
any of my publications who can say I have ever fooled or
tricked them. I have given you the chance to see for yourself—decide for yourselves—refute or support me if you
can.'

*   *   *

The fourth and most recent photograph of the hole at the
North Pole is rather more problematical, although poten-
tially it offers the most exciting confirmation of the Hollow
Earth theory. The source and the date when it was taken
are less certain than those of 1967 and 1968, but it has been
widely disseminated and discussed on the Internet during
the past few years.

The most generally held view is that the picture was taken
by the Apollo 16 spacecraft shortly after its launch on 20
April, 1972. This Moon mission was completed on 27 April
when the spacecraft and crew safely splashed down in the
Pacific Ocean. A huge selection of photographs taken by the
spacecraft and its crew were subsequently made available to
the media, but it was not until several years later that the
image in question was spotted among the batch. It showed
a full view of planet Earth, with close to the top a circular
opening amidst the cloud cover of the North Pole.

The picture had been processed at the Goddard Flight
Centre in New Mexico, but not released to the NASA Photo-
graphic Library until the mid-Seventies. Why this delay
occurred can now only be a matter for conjecture. However,
because all NASA material is designated in the public

domain, it was at once available for publication and was soon being reprinted and discussed in several small-circulation American and Australian publications devoted to Fortean topics. Despite this, the existence of the photograph was not generally realised until it was posted on a web-site, 'Space Images', in 1996.

Since that date the site has attracted many hundreds of curious visitors, not to mention a continuing debate about the picture's authenticity . . . or otherwise. The photograph has also been computer-enlarged and enhanced around the area of the North Pole, and the copy included in this book is one of the largest available. It shows what appears to be a completely snow-free landmass just inside the rim of the hole. Only partly obscured by clouds are what are believed to be waves breaking around the entranceway. One American Hollow Earth researcher has commented on the fact that the hole seems to be an almost perfect circle, and he wonders if the particular dispersement of the clouds across it indicates that there is a warm atmosphere just below— as has so often been suggested.

Naturally, what all the visitors to the 'Space Images' site really want to know is this: if the photograph is genuine, *why* is such a great discovery being kept secret? Jan Lamprecht, who has written literally thousands of words on the Hollow Earth, is in no doubt.

I have long held the opinion—and many will hate me for saying this—but UFOlogy is going nowhere. People are rushing down the wrong path, watching Area 51, chasing reptilians, looking at crop circles and trying to catch cattle mutes [mutilators]. No big coverup is needed because people are already looking in the wrong place for the wrong thing. Back in the early days, researchers and the US Government were on even ground, but the Government's successful silencing campaign has made the need for silencing less and less today.

The fact is, the Earth is hollow and an advanced civilisation may be on our doorstep. The few who dare go against the grain and believe this are the only ones the Government are really interested in. They are the only people who actually stand a chance of upsetting the cart. I have no doubt that as one gets closer to the truth, the US Government will begin to play rough.

Although I cannot altogether subscribe to Jan Lamprecht's rather alarmist views, I *do* believe there is evidence to support his contention—and that of a number of other researchers including, of course, Ray Palmer and Brinsley Le Poer Trench—that UFOs originate from inside the earth. The evidence that I have assembled of sightings from both the North and South Poles also points to this conclusion.

Nine

UFOs FROM THE HOLLOW EARTH—1
The Antarctic

The first of the series of 'cigar-shaped' flying objects in the sky were witnessed during the last week of July 1909. They moved 'at a great velocity' and were seen during the day and at night when, apparently, lights emanating from inside made them visible to dozens of people on the ground. For the next six weeks, until the first week of September, the mystery sightings continued almost every day until, as dramatically as they had begun, the objects were seen no more. Only one fact about the visitation, if such it was, remained incontrovertible: all the UFOs had been seen approaching from, or going away to, *the south* where, as every eyewitness knew, lay the impenetrable mystery of Antarctica.

These extraordinary events which occurred ninety years ago over New Zealand's South Island and, in particular, over the town of Invercargill, are remarkable for three reasons. First, the only flying machines in the world at that time were those of Count Zeppelin, who had launched his first dirigible in Germany in 1900, and the Wright Brothers, who had taken to the air at Kitty Hawk in 1903. Although airships were in use in Europe from 1909, their range was strictly limited and none could have flown to New Zealand—much less with the speed and manoeuvrability demonstrated by these mystery craft! Second, in 1909 the terms UFO and 'Flying Saucer' had not been coined, and such reports as there had been about mysterious sightings in the heavens were generally put down to freaks of the weather, mirages or illusions. And third, this is the earliest report on record lending weight to the idea that the UFOs which have been seen all over the world may *not* originate from space, as many experts would like to believe, but from the Hollow Earth, which they enter and leave via the North and South Poles. In this chapter we shall be examining almost a century of evidence from the nations closest to the Antarctic, which add credibility to this hypothesis. In the next, the focus will be on the Arctic region.

Invercargill, where the story begins, stands behind Bluff Harbour on the southernmost part of South Island. Facing the harbour is Stewart Island, shaped like an arrowhead pointing directly towards the South Pole. It is mentioned as a landmark in a number of the accounts about the cigar-shaped objects, which were also described as 'torpedo', 'codfish' or 'boat'-shaped. Several of them were reported elsewhere on South Island, and a handful were even observed over North Island. These accounts from dozens of witnesses, which were gathered by the New Zealand press, all confirmed the same basic facts. The 'phantoms' varied their pace from hovering to shooting across the sky at enormous speed. They were all majestic in flight, rising and falling like birds on the wing, and able to manoeuvre in tight circles, sometimes coming as close as 1,000 feet to the ground.

In September 1909, after the wave of sightings had ended, an article in the *Christchurch Press* reported a particularly unusual occurrence in the town of Gore, less than 40 miles from Invercargill.

Two local residents of Gore reported having seen, at night, a boat-shaped object carrying two large fans and three lights—which at times were covered by the fans. Two other residents (dredge hands) in the same locality reported an object shaped like a boat with an open top that came down through the mist in the early morning. The dredge hands swear they could discern two figures on board the craft. A similar object was seen by several schoolchildren at noon on the same day. They stated it had the figure of a man seated in it. And the manager of a firm in Invercargill observed a cigar-shaped object which moved along the coast, five miles from the shore. He said he watched it for 15 minutes before it made off majestically towards the South Pole.

Understandably, these curious incidents on South Island have continued to attract the interest of UFO researchers. Henk J. Hinfelaar, the director of the New Zealand Scientific Space Research Centre and editor of the magazine *Spaceview*, has compiled his own dossier of the events and wrote recently: 'There is no evidence to suggest that the year 1909 produced any UFO landings in New Zealand. To most witnesses the six-week flurry of sightings was, however, convincing enough to accept that intelligently controlled alien craft of an unknown identity had been visiting New Zealand skies.'

These Antarctica-bound UFOs were to prove the first of many that have since been seen not only over New Zealand, but also over other countries in this part of the world.

Just three years later, in 1912, a resident of Dunedin, some miles up the east coast from Invercargill, saw another mystery object. An account of this, by Isabella Walmsley of Christchurch, was quoted by Harold T. Wilkins in his book *Flying Saucers on the Moon* (1954). Mrs Walmsley also referred to an experience of her own, some years later.

Everybody, of course, thought this man in Dunedin was a bit 'touched' when he claimed to have seen a strange object in the sky going south along the coast. He must have seen a meteor, folks said ... Now, I am a light sleeper, a legacy from my days as a nurse, and one night, when we were living in Timaru [also along the coast about 100 miles from Dunedin], I was awakened, suddenly, by a loud, roaring, hissing noise that passed swiftly over the house. It was the year 1935, before there were night-flying planes here. When the Second World War broke out, I thought it must have been a Jap plane, but it did not occur to me to wonder where the base of such a rover could be, with thousands of miles of open sea all around New Zealand! A few days later, I was talking to an old chap who lived in the neighbourhood and he told me that he had to get up in the night, and when he got outside into the open air he saw a 'big light like the sun, moving south over your house, missie!'

In April 1952, I spent a week in Dunedin and was similarly wakened by a loud swish overhead going south. It was still, and about 4 a.m. There was no fading. The noise was there, and then it wasn't! I did not mention it to the people I was living with as I knew how they could regard the story. A few days later, the New Zealand and Australian newspapers were full of flying saucer stories.

In 1955–6 three more incidents were reported, all by pilots familiar with any *normal* kind of craft flying in the skies of New Zealand. Again the UFOs were all travelling on a direct south-north line from the Antarctic. On 31 October, the captain of a National Airlines DC-3 on its way from Wellington to Christchurch reported a 'bright, round object' which flew directly overhead and down the coast of South Island.

The following year, on the night of Sunday, 10 June, Leading Aircraftsman B. L. Lovelock was walking along the road at Waikumete when he saw what he described as 'an upturned saucer with a bell-shaped dome on top'. The UFO was bluish white in colour, Lovelock said, and he watched it for some time before it headed towards the southern horizon. The Leading Aircraftsman added that he had 'an uncomfortable feeling of being seized up by the flying saucer' which has led to speculation that he might have been the victim of an unsuccessful alien abduction.

On 3 September of that same year, two pilots of No. 4 Transport Squadron of the Royal New Zealand Air Force reported a similar incident. Squadron-Leader K. B. Smith, the commanding officer of the squadron, was flying a Hastings across South Island at 6.42 p.m. when he saw 'a glowing object' heading in the direction of Dunedin. 'At first I thought it was a jet,' said the Squadron-Leader, 'but then I realised it was not. The thing was travelling on a horizontal plane at a fantastic speed.' Smith said that he later learned that one of his colleagues, Squadron-Leader O. Staples, had also seen the UFO.

On 5 April, 1960 there was a return visit to Invercargill of a 'strange flying object' according to the *Wellington Evening Post*. The circular craft with flashing lights was seen by eyewitnesses travelling low over the estuary towards Bluff Harbour and disappeared in the direction of the Antarctic, reviving memories among older residents of the 1909 sightings.

Palmerston, on the coast just to the north of Dunedin, was the location for a sighting on 16 June, 1963, when a college student, Harold Fulton, saw 'two brilliant lights descending in a zig-zag fashion.' The objects remained stationary for about five seconds, 'then suddenly shot off at very great speed, at first in level flight across my front, and climbed up into the sky at approximately 45 degrees.' His last glimpse of the pair of lights was disappearing to the south.

A more recent, well-publicised New Zealand sighting, which also pinpoints a UFO heading for the Antarctic, occurred in January 1979 when Captain J. Startup, flying an RNZAF Skyhawk jet fighter, saw a bright, oval-shaped object going south over Cook Strait between South and North Islands. 'No aircraft could have accelerated as that thing did,' he said when he was back on ground. Geoffrey Causer, an air traffic controller, logged this UFO and a number of others during the same period and commented, 'They were unidentified flying somethings. They were definitely not planes and that's the only thing I can be definite on. We have recorded sightings by six pilots on three Argosy aircraft over ten days and a host of radar sightings. There is obviously some strange phenomenon going on around South Island and it needs to be investigated.'

There is similar evidence available in Australia of UFO activity to and from the pole. Here again the tradition predates stories of 'Flying Saucers', and one of the earliest accounts is by a very impressive eyewitness, Sir Francis Chichester, the famous yachtsman. Prior to his lone crossings of the Atlantic, Chichester was well known for his daring flights in a Tiger Moth. On 10 June, 1931, he took off from New South Wales to fly to New Zealand. From the open cockpit of his tiny plane he had a perfect view across clear blue sky and sea. Suddenly, from the direction of the Antarctic, he saw what looked like a dull grey-white airship approaching. 'It was like an oblong pearl,' he said later to the magazine *The Unknown*, 'flashing brightly, periodically vanishing, reappearing, accelerating and finally disappearing back the way it had come.' And he went on:

I screwed up my eyes, unable to believe them, and twisted the plane this way and that, thinking that the object must be hidden by a blind spot. Dazzling flashes continued in four or five different places, but I still could not pick out any planes. Then, out of some clouds to my right front, I saw another, or possibly the same, advancing. I watched it intently, determined not to look away for a fraction of a second. It drew closer and I could see the dull gleam of light on its nose and back. It came on, but instead of increasing in size, it diminished as it approached. When quite near, it suddenly became its own ghost—one second I could see through it, and the next it had vanished. Whatever it was I saw, it seems to have been very much like what people have since claimed to be flying saucers.

Twenty years later, another level-headed commercial pilot, Captain B. L. Jones, flying for Australian Northern Airways, saw an equally puzzling object off the coast of Queensland near Brisbane on the evening of 17 May 1953. 'It appeared to have a glass dome brightly illuminated, and beamed a dazzling light. It was noiseless, manoeuvred round my 'plane and twice crossed my path. An aircraft control tower check-up showed no other aircraft near. Nine hours later a radio operator saw it over the Pacific ascending at a great velocity in the direction of the South Pole.'

In 1954 a series of 'Flying Saucer' stories gripped the Australian media, the majority of these observed over the southernmost state of Victoria, especially around Melbourne. On 1 January, for instance, thousands of racegoers at Hanging Rock, saw 'a round, silvery disc hanging stationary and noiselessly in the sky for two minutes before turning on its edge and vanishing south.' Stranger still, on the same day, people on Hampton Beach observed a 'clear plastic-like object, like a dish, rush across the skyline', while in various other parts of the state 'a huge silver object of unknown origin trailing a streamer of red-blue flame' was seen moving at an amazing speed in a southerly direction. On 6 January, after twenty more sightings over Victoria, including six at Melbourne, the Superintendent of Traffic Control in the Department of Civil Aviation appealed for reports of UFOs from the public, 'They are *not* a joke,' he insisted. (He was probably *not* amused, however, when he received a letter on 14 January from an unnamed French professor of science who claimed that 'flying saucers in opposed cohorts will fight out the next world war: black Jupes, or Jupiterians on one side, and Red Martians on the other, with our old planet as their football.')

On Sunday, 19 May, 1957, occurred what is still described as 'one of the most authenticated UFO sightings in Australia' when a 'silver-coloured object leaving a white vapour trail flew at speeds in excess of 2,000 mph across the State of Victoria heading south.' Telephone switchboards at Melbourne's weather bureau, police headquarters, airline and newspaper offices were jammed with phone calls from 5.45 p.m. to 8 p.m. when an estimated 2,300 sightings were reported from hundreds of miles apart. Among the eyewitnesses one account is particularly significant: that of several crews of fishermen on the Tasman Sea. They described the high-flying silvery object as being 'like a fish' and heading 'straight for the South Pole'. That night, two Meteor jet fighters were put on stand-by in case the UFO returned.

The year 1960 brought another curious report which fits into the same pattern. On 3 October, 'six flying saucers and a "mother ship"' were reported over Tasmania. A Church of England minister on the island said he had first seen the mysterious craft nearly a week earlier, but was reluctant to report them until other people in the area told the same story. All agreed that the objects appeared and disappeared *to the south*. A similar account of a mother ship and small objects over the coast of South Australia in 1961 is reported in detail by Jacques Vallee in his *Anatomy of a Phenomenon* (1965). A group of round, silvery objects was observed leaving and returning to a bigger object which finally collected them all and departed at high speed southwards over the Great Australian Bight.

Australia had another bumper year of sightings in 1965, starting on 25 July when a number of children in Melbourne reported a bright, silvery object that manoeuvred in the sky above them, rose vertically, gave off bright flashes, and then disappeared out to sea. A metallic disc was also observed racing to the southern horizon from Australia's farthest-flung territory, Macquarie Island, in November.

By far the most extraordinary story to come from Australia, however, occurred over the Bass Strait between Melbourne and Tasmania on 21 October, 1978, when a pilot was lost in what is alleged to have been a UFO abduction. In the early evening, 20-year-old Frederick Valentich set out in his single-engined Cessna 182 on a short solo flight from Melbourne to King Island. He was about 95 miles southwest of Melbourne when he reported to ground control on the mainland that he was being followed by 'a high-speed object with green lights'. Asked by a controller to identify the craft as there was no other traffic in the area, Valentich insisted it was not an aircraft. After a brief break in transmission, the pilot came back on the air again: 'It's coming for me now. I'm orbiting [circling] and the thing is orbiting on top of me also ... it has a green light and sort of metallic light on the outside.' At this, a long metallic noise was heard and Valentich and his plane vanished without a trace.

Two other light aircraft have also disappeared in mysterious circumstances while flying over the Bass Strait. In December 1969, a Fuji single-engined aircraft with only the pilot on board was lost on a flight to King Island; and in

September 1972, a Tiger Moth with two people on board vanished on a similar trip from the mainland. After extensive and fruitless searches, the official explanation was that all three pilots had probably confused the lights with 'the planet Venus . . . which is very bright at this time.' The statement was greeted with understandable scepticism, even ridicule. What no one was able to explain was that in each case the UFOs had first been seen materialising from *due south*.

I have also discovered evidence that the South Pole may be the point of origin for UFOs in a number of sightings from the Cape Province of South Africa and Argentina which were reported in *Flying Saucer Review*.

Probably the earliest report of a UFO in South Africa came in May 1953, when a circular-shaped object, glowing brightly, was tracked from north to south across the country and was last seen heading away over the most southerly point, Cape Agulhas, at 'over a thousand miles an hour'. At Upington, also in Cape Province, on 7 December the following year, a meteorologist reported tracking a 'hemispherical object' which moved at tremendous speed as it disappeared over the Indian Ocean. The 'mysterious orange-red object shaped like a yo-yo', which also shot out to sea over Durban in March 1956 after being observed by four different people, was believed to have been about 50 feet in diameter with windows 'from which a reddish light shone'.

Farther south along the coast at East London, in July 1956 a 'scarlet fireball' was seen in the sky by a number of eyewitnesses. Mr W. Whyte was in Tapson Street with his family where 'the glare gradually died out as it drifted at a fairly low level from north to south'. The following year, on 1 November, 1957, two Sabre jet fighters of the South African Air Force were sent up to investigate dozens of reports of two cylindrical-shaped objects which had come in across the coast of Natal, swung over Pretoria and Johannesburg 'at enormous speed' and then headed off south. The pilot of one of the jets radioed that when he climbed to his maximum height of more than 45,000 feet, the two objects were ahead of him several thousand feet higher 'and going in the direction of the Antarctic'. An Air Force intelligence officer told the press, 'We can only assume that the objects were some form of physical phenomena for which we have, as yet, no explanation.'

The report of a 'flying saucer' hovering for over four hours near Fort Beaufort on the Eastern Cape in June 1972 is one of the most remarkable accounts from South Africa and equally significant in terms of our hypothesis. On June 27 what was described as 'an oval object, gun-metal in colour, that glowed and frequently changed colour from green to yellow to white', was seen by Bernie Smith over his land, Braeside Farm. For much of the morning the object was observed by Mr Smith and several of his African workers 'criss-crossing the sky as if it was studying us,' as the farmer said later when a team of police officers arrived to investigate. By then, however, the object had flown off 'with a terrific rush of speed heading south'.

A similar pattern of reports has emerged from Argentina, dating from the same period. Once again, a significant number of them state that the UFOs flew off in a southerly direction. In November 1954, a meteorologist working at Grande Bay near the southern tip of the country observed through his binoculars 'two, hovering, luminous objects' which passed over the Falkland Islands going towards the pole. Three years later, in July 1957, a group of local dignitaries at Comodoro Rivadavia on the Gulf of San Jorge glimpsed a 'brilliant object' heading across the sea towards them. Dr Hugo Zamit and lawyer Manuel Altuna were driving in a car at the time and saw the UFO change course several times before disappearing 'faster than any known earthly contrivance'. Two days later, the mayor of Comodoro Rivadavia and some of his councillors reported seeing an identical object hovering over the coast before speeding away across the South Atlantic Ocean.

In the spring of 1962 it was the turn of the Argentine navy to see strange objects in the sky. According to the Buenos Aires newspaper *El Mundo*, four sightings were made at sea—two by naval pilots and two by ships' officers. Later the same paper reported that on the night of 15 June at Mar del Plata, a number of people saw 'an extraordinary bright object flying high in the sky', while at the neighbouring coastal resort of Miramar a cigar-shaped object was seen at 9.30 p.m. flying in from the direction of the South Atlantic. The whole craft was vividly illuminated, *El Mundo* said, and carried three very bright lights—red in the centre, yellow on the right, and green on the left. 'The flood of these cosmic sightings of late has had a profound emotional impact on the many eyewitnesses,' the paper added, 'and may well mark a new era with regard to the UFO problem [sic].'

Two subsequent events in Argentina have also earned considerable media attention and comment. On 17 July, 1965, a circular object which 'reflected the rays of the sun on its metallic and polished surface' hovered over a beach near the River Plata, where it was seen by hundreds of bathers and prompted a demand from *La Nacion* the following day: 'We do not believe the true explanations of such occurrences can be kept secret much longer.'

The same paper—in company with a number of others in South America—carried an even more sensational story about truck driver Vicente Bordoli of Mar del Plata, and what happened to him on 12 August, 1982 while he was driving southwards along National Highway No. 3. This road skirts the South Atlantic coast of Argentina, and as Bordoli was driving along with his son, Hugo, he caught sight of a strange, luminous craft hovering over the sea. He pulled over to the side of the road and father and son watched the object closely.

'I have heard all about flying saucers,' Bordoli later told the press. 'And I am sure this was one. It remained stationary in the air for several minutes before diving down towards the horizon. I am absolutely certain that it is in the depths of the sea somewhere that these flying saucers have their base.'

*   *   *

One of the first UFOlogists to hint at the significance of all these sightings in the vicinity of the South Pole was Brinsley Le Poer Trench in an article he wrote for *Flying Saucer Review* of May–June, 1956: 'Does Antarctica Hold the Key?'

It is no good trying to evaluate flying saucers and their occupants on the basis of present knowledge. So, then, is it a 'way-out' extension of the theory about them to say that if the centre of the earth is hollow with vast openings in the polar regions, they might originate from there? Saucers have, of course, been reported over many countries in the world, but especially the polar regions. It would seem that parts of South America, Australia, New Zealand and South Africa have all had a large crop of UFO activity. So does the key to it all lie in the frozen wastes of the Continent surrounding the South Pole?

A series of articles in the popular Brazilian magazine *O Cruziero* at the same time revealed that others were also thinking along the same lines. In this instance the writer was Paulo Strauss, a former Commander in the Brazilian Navy, whose article 'Flying Saucers from a Subterranean World' was published in the February 1956 issue:

The hypothesis of the extra-terrestrial origin of flying saucers does not seem acceptable. Another possibility is that they are military aircraft belonging to some existing nation on earth, but no one possesses such a technology. So we must consider the most recent and interesting theory that has been offered to account for the origin of flying saucers: the existence of a great Subterranean World with perhaps innumerable cities in which live people who have reached a very high degree of civilisation, economic organisation and social, cultural and spiritual development together with extraordinary scientific progress, in comparison with whom the humanity that lives on the earth's surface may be considered as a race of barbarians.

Another group of investigators in America, the International Flying Saucer Bureau, based in Connecticut, are more inclined to the view that Antarctica is probably some kind of base, as Le Poer Trench noted in his 1956 article:

They ask if it is not possible that space visitors might already be here and have established a base in Antarctica? The continent is unknown, unexplored and unpopulated. It is an ideal place for alien flying saucers to condition themselves to our atmosphere . . . a place where their activities would go unobserved for the most part, but not altogether. Another factor which may have some bearing on the South Pole theme is that saucers may possibly be powered by some type of force field that has a direct effect on gravity. The South Magnetic Pole may be an ideal place for charging up with this power.

Le Poer Trench concluded his ground-breaking article by citing two authenticated sightings which he believed supported his theory. In March 1950, while cruising in Antarctic waters, a Chilean naval officer, Commander Augusto Vars Orrego, reported, 'During the night, which is very bright in these parts, we saw flying saucers, one above the other, turning at tremendous speeds. We have photographs to prove what we saw.' Annoyingly, these pictures have never been released by the Chilean naval authorities, despite repeated requests. Six years later, in January 1956, a group of scientists who had been flown to Robertson Island in the Weddell Sea to study the island's geology observed 'two metallic, cigar-shaped objects reflected in the rays of the sun'. These craft performed a series of high-speed, acute-angle changes of direction which led the eye-witnesses to believe they were 'being spied upon by an intelligence that for some reason or other desired to remain anonymous'. As suddenly as they had appeared, the UFOs disappeared beyond the horizon.

In the years since Le Poer Trench's article was published, several more sightings have occurred at the South Pole which lend more weight to his conclusions. In 1958, during International Geophysical Year, when scientists from eleven countries built dozens of research stations and camps across the continent to carry out surveys, it was a case of one odd occurrence after another, as Peter Kolosimo has described in his book *Not of this World* (1970):

From the workers around the Argentinian stations there came at least a dozen stories of seeing unidentified objects in the sky or on the ice, most of them having oval shapes. Various Russian and American investigators flew over areas full of structures odd enough to make them think of open spaces with gigantic walls and buildings covered in heavy slabs of ice. Some attached to the Soviet bases (probably Vostok One, Two or Sovietskaya) said they had seen structures which were 'too geometrical' to be accounted for by weathering; and even 'things moving', among them being a squat, dark, creeping mass of something and a white shape similar to that of the bear or human being.

An eyewitness account of an encounter in Antarctica at this time will be found in Chapter Eleven of the present book.

Kolosimo picked up where Le Poer Trench had left off to re-emphasise just how frequently sightings of UFOs occurred in the Antarctic. He made a particular point of an incident in July 1965 which was so unusual as to generate an official statement. The story had originated in the Brazilian newspaper *O Estado de Sao Paulo*, and I quote from its issue of 8 July:

For the first time in history, an official communiqué has been published by the government about flying saucers. It is a document from the Argentine Navy, based on the statements of a large number of Argentine, Chilean and British sailors stationed in the naval base in Antarctica. The communiqué reads: 'The Argentine garrison in Argentinian Antarctic (Deception Island) noticed on July 3rd at 19.14 hours (local time) a huge lens-shaped flying object; it seemed to be solid, of a reddish-green colour chiefly, sometimes changing to a yellow, blue, white or orange shade. The object moved in a zigzag towards the east, but changed course several times towards the west and north at varying speeds and quite silently, passing at 45 degrees over the horizon at a distance of 10 to 15 kilometres from the base. In the course of the movement completed by the object itself it was possible for the eye-witnesses to get some idea of its enormous speed, and not only because it was poised motionless for about 15 minutes at a height of around 5,000 metres.'

The Secretariat of the Argentine Navy also states in its communiqué that the occurrence was witnessed by scientists of the three naval bases and that the facts described by these people agree completely. It is understood that the photographs taken by a photographer at one of these bases will be made public after they have been analysed by scientists. [Once again, this intention has never been carried out.]

Since then, reports of unidentified objects have continued to come in from the vast wilderness. In March 1971, for example, the crew of an ice-breaker at work in Admiralty Bay saw overhead 'a multicoloured fireball-like object'; while in June 1983 it was the turn of some meteorologists working in Prydz Bay to spot a disc-like object that glistened in the sun as it streaked inland. Most recently, in July 1993, yellow-white discs were observed flying at enormous speed over Cape Hallett. According to a later report, 'As the last of these objects neared the horizon [on 11 July], it disappeared in the auroral glow.'

The sheer weight of this evidence can, surely, lead to only one conclusion, as Pierre Deville wrote in *Aurora* in March 1980:

There is something to look for down there! But what? Perhaps a fantastic astroport, maintained for countless millennia in what was once a marvellous continent and is now a chaos of ice? Let us remember that for centuries prior to the discovery of Antarctica an unknown number of adventurers, navigators and dreamers pushed down southwards seeking the 'southern paradise' sometimes called 'Rainbow City' which was supposed to have been built before the Flood in materials all the colours of the rainbow. They were not simply following some personal fancy but being guided by records of a myth surviving for hundreds of thousands of years!

Not long after this article, in 1983, a respected American scientist confirmed that *something* did exist at the South Pole—a gigantic crater. But according to Professor John G. Weihaupt of Indiana University, the hole was not a natural formation but the result of a gigantic meteorite striking the earth. Although still undiscovered, he said, the crater was about half a mile deep, 150 miles wide and lay hidden beneath the ice of northern Antarctica. In his estimation, the hole had been caused by a meteorite weighing around 13 billion tons and measuring 2.5 to 3.75 miles across, which had collided with the earth between 600,000 to 700,000 years ago at a speed of 44,000 miles per hour. A crater of such a size, however, would be more than *four times* larger than any other meteorite hole ever found on this planet and such an impact could well change the earth's axis or rotation. A much simpler explanation of Professor Weihaupt's 'hole' might be that it is the entranceway to the inner world. The dimensions, as the reader will have noticed, are uncannily similar.

Shortly before his death in 1995, Brinsley Le Poer Trench, who had initiated so much of the speculation about UFOs originating from the South Pole, hazarded a guess about just *where* the entrance might be that UFOs used to enter and leave the interior world. Writing in *Flying Saucer Review* he stated:

I believe the South Pole opening is in the region on the map of Antarctica known as 'The Area of Inaccessibility'. It covers a very large area of rough terrain but the reason for its name is because of navigational problems. The magnetic compass is useless and the inertial guidance system does not function either. It is possible to reach the geographical South Pole through inertial guidance, but *not* the hole in 'The Area of Inaccessibility'. The entrance is some distance from the South Pole, anything from 600 to 1,800 miles. It is similar in size to the hole beyond the so-called North Pole—that is, not more than 285 miles in diameter and not less than 50. *There* lies the answer to one of the great secrets of the ages.

In the next chapter we shall look at the evidence for the equally frequent sightings of UFOs in the Arctic Circle; and, in particular, we shall investigate the story of a mysterious crash of an object which, in its own way, is as strange and significant an event as the famous 'Roswell Incident' in New Mexico in 1947.

Ten

UFOs FROM THE
HOLLOW EARTH—2
The Arctic Circle

There is a remarkable resemblance between the reports of
UFOs observed flying in the direction of the North Pole
and those described in the last chapter on the approaches
to Antarctica. Here, at the northernmost part of the world,
more than half a century of eyewitness accounts indicates
a similarly large number of strange objects traversing the
Arctic Circle and, in so doing, adding further weight to
the conviction that flying saucers originate from *inside* the
Earth.

A number of territories surround the North Pole—
Canada, Alaska, Russia, Scandinavia and Greenland—and
before considering the implications of what may lie at their
heart deep inside the Arctic region, we need to look at the
most significant of the UFO reports. What follows are by
no means all the eyewitness accounts that I have collected
during my research, merely those that are typical and from
the most widely distant locations.

North America makes an ideal starting-point as, here
again, UFOs were seen years before the popular term for
them was invented. In the earliest-known instance, on the
night of 9 February, 1913, the objects which sped across
the continent took the form of 'a procession of strange,

weaving lights'. Subsequently, a dossier of eyewitness reports on the phenomenon was compiled by Professor John Chant of Toronto, who wrote in the *Journal of the Royal Astronomical Society of Canada* in November of that same year:

> A strange spectacle was noticed sweeping across Canada (over Saskatchewan and Ontario), the USA (New York) and thereafter over the Atlantic Ocean heading northward. A luminous body was seen, with a long tail attached to it. The body grew rapidly larger. Observers differed as to whether this body was single, or in three or four parts, with a tail to each. The group, or complex structure, moved with a peculiar, *majestic* deliberation [see the Invercargill report in Chapter Nine for comparison].

Other observers whose stories Professor Chant collected said that the 'weird bodies' moved in groups 'rather like a fleet of battleships attended by cruisers and destroyers'. One viewer, W. F. Denning, a New York astrologer who saw the UFOs heading north from the end of Long Island, said that they followed the curvature of the earth 'as no meteorite would do', adding, 'Some people I know said they looked like airships cruising over the city, but I have never seen anything like it in all my years of studying the heavens.' Another writer to the *Journal* thought that there had probably been as many as 30 objects in all 'and so perfect was their lining up you would have thought it was an aerial fleet manoeuvring.'

Just eighteen years later, a solitary 'bright light' was seen making a similar sweep across the skies of Canada. This UFO was first spotted at dawn on the morning of 1 January, 1931, by a group of people in Cobden, Ontario. The object 'flashed' as it sped across the sky in a great curve which took it away north across the Hudson Bay. One observer of the phenomenon told the *Ottawa Journal* he felt the sight was 'like something out of a tale by Jules Verne or H. G. Wells!'

In the late Forties and Fifties, Goose Bay in Labrador was the centre for a whole series of 'flying saucer' sightings, all of which were observed travelling in the direction of the Arctic Circle. On 31 October, 1948, a 'strange object' was tracked by radar travelling at over 600 mph and, according to a report made at the time, was of a type known to the authorities as an 'angel' or low altitude signal from some invisible object. 'Not astral,' the statement added significantly.

On 19 June, 1952, a 'reddish object' was observed from Goose Bay crossing the night sky at a very high speed. Much the same phenomenon appeared again going north on 15 December that year, although this time it changed to 'a whitish colour while manoeuvring'. Probably the most striking encounter in this area occurred on 30 June, 1954, when the crew and passengers of a Canadian Airlines flight over Goose Bay saw 'a large UFO with several smaller satellite objects' which they observed for several minutes as the procession flew high above them towards the Arctic regions.

In the Fifties, several sightings of UFOs were reported from Newfoundland, all northward bound. The two most significant of these were from an eyewitness on the ground and another in the air. On 1 February, 1950, at St John's, Pat Walsh, a telephone company electrician, reported seeing a 'tear-shaped object as bright as a fluorescent light' race over the town and head out to sea. He said it was in sight for at least twelve seconds and appeared to be following 'an arch-like flight' at an extremely high speed. Among others who saw the UFO was a Mrs C. Vaughan who told the *Newfoundland Evening Telegram* that as it crossed the town she thought she saw a dome on the top. Six years later, in June 1956, the pilot of a naval transport aircraft reported being 'paced' by a large, disc-shaped craft as it flew over Gander.

So numerous were the sightings of unidentified objects over Canada during the following twelve months that on 22 July, 1957, the Canadian Broadcasting Service ran a special news bulletin reporting, 'Ground observer corps of the Royal Canadian Air Force have been tracking UFOs in the skies over Ontario for the past month. The chief observer in the Don Mills area, Toronto, Mr Herbert Harrison, described these objects as like little balls of fire moving from north to east, east to west and then from west to north before disappearing. He said the Corps had no idea what they were, but they would continue to maintain a close watch on the mystery lights.'

In the Seventies and Eighties a significant number of UFO sightings over Canada occurred in the North Bay area, where again they virtually all appeared or disappeared in a northerly direction. The RCAF once more investigated these sightings of 'orange/red discs' which were tracked 'flying extremely high, zig-zagging, and making complex manoeuvres at very high speeds.'

The US Air Force also took an interest in these sightings, especially because a number occurred close to Alaska, the 'detached' state of America. Here, too, a search of the records reveals that UFOs have been reported over the state for half a century, most originating from the Arctic Circle.

Stories of unidentified objects over Alaska began in the last year of the Second World War. In 1945, near the Aleutian Islands, 14 men on an attack transport, the USAT *Delarof*, reported seeing a dark, spherical object which arose over the northern horizon, circled the ship, and then flew back the same way. Several of the crew were apparently convinced the UFO had actually risen out of the sea. An official report of the incident was sent to Washington, but no further details have been made public.

Secrecy also surrounds another incident which happened in the late Forties. In May 1948, a film cameraman working for the government in Alaska was told by some Inuit of 'strange discs in the skies' which, they said, came from 'the great land to the North'. Subsequently the man took some pictures of these lights, but when he returned to the States his employers—the US Government—took possession of the film and deposited it in a vault in Los Angeles where it has remained to this day.

On 2 December, 1950, while a Reeves Airway pilot, C. G. Kelley, was approaching an airfield eight miles southwest of Anchorage, he suddenly noticed an object overhead travelling at great speed, its brightness increasing in intensity until it was too blinding to look at. 'Then there was a kind of explosion,' Kelly later told newspapermen in Fairbanks, 'and the object vanished in a northeasterly direction.' The UFO was also reported across an area from Kodiak to Fairbanks and specifically at Seward, Portage, Skwentna and Anchorage, 'where anti-aircraft batteries opened fire on the object as it whizzed overhead,' according to one account.

Two years later, on 22 January, 1952, another strange object was tracked on radar over North Alaska, which resulted in the sending up of three F-94 interceptors to investigate, and on 14 February a group of airline employees at Nome saw a silvery rocket-like object with an orange flame trail manoeuvring 'as if it were manned and controlled'. A similar object was also sighted at Unalakleet on the same day, *moving rapidly northwest* leaving contrails behind.

An even more extraordinary story found its way into the press in February 1969. Lee R. Munsick, a former director of NICAP, told the *New York Daily News* on 19 February that UFOs had actually been seen 'landing and manoeuvring' in northern Alaska and the North Pole area during the previous two weeks. 'The Alaskan sighting involved a single disc-shaped craft that was seen by a party of trappers about 200 miles east of Umiat,' Munsick said. 'The men estimated the UFO was about two miles away when they first noticed it. The craft rose and descended to within a few feet of the ground several times, then flew slowly in a tight circle before disappearing. The men said the object was red-coloured.'

This same phenomenon had been reported by two Norwegian soldiers in the area of the McKinlay Sea, Munsick added. 'They noticed a saucer-shaped object which seemed to rise form the direction of the North Pole and fly away in the direction of Greenland. The object moved with great speed. One of the men thought he saw it later fly back towards the Pole.'

However, the most famous UFO report in Alaska occurred in November 1986 when a Japanese airline pilot, Captain Kenjyu Terauchi, described what he and his crew saw while flying a JAL 747 jumbo jet at 35,000 feet above the Alaskan tundra en route from Iceland to Anchorage. Terauchi said they were suddenly aware of 'two bright lights moving sporadically 600 metres below us and to our left, like two bear cubs playing.' This was followed by a brilliant light shining directly into the cockpit, while in front was the discernible outline of a craft.

'Its shape was squarish, flying 500–1,000 feet in front of us, very slightly higher in altitude,' the Captain said. 'Its size was about the same as the body of a DC-8 jet and with numerous exhaust pipes. The firing of the exhaust jets varied, perhaps to maintain balance. From the craft several tiny bright objects detached themselves and flew in formation parallel to the 747.'

After about a minute, the bright objects were reunited with the 'mother' craft and it disappeared to the north.

Throughout the 'close encounter', interference made it impossible for the JAL captain to contact Anchorage Air Control, but when he did get through he was told that nothing whatsoever had been seen on the radar. On landing, Terauchi and his crew gave a full account to the Federal Aviation Authority which concluded that they had all been 'professional and rational' about everything they saw. The mystery of JAL Flight 1628 still remains unsolved.

For many years, no reports of UFOs or flying saucers were forthcoming from North America's neighbour, the former Soviet Union. However, in the British newspaper *The Sunday Times* of 5 March, 1961, in an article headlined 'Russia Bars Talk of Flying Saucers', reporter Marvin Kalb in Moscow wrote, 'In fact, stories about them had begun as early as 1949 when a Polar scientist named Murashov took a picture of a "strange object of unusual form" which seemed to be "some fantastic flying apparatus".'

Significantly, the earliest stories of flying saucers had come primarily from 'the far north of Russia', and ranged from serious accounts reported from Bolshevik Island, of 'speeding bright lights' seen over the Arctic Ocean, to a far-fetched yarn of 'Martian pygmies landing in Siberia'. One story even spoke of the arrival in the far north of 'a green creature from outer space'.

Gossip reached such a pitch, said Kalb, that the Communist Party newspaper *Pravda* approached Academician L. A. Artsimovich of the Moscow Society for the Dissemination of Scientific and Political Information, to denounce the rumours and launch a crusade against 'all such anti-scientific information'. Artsimovich took to his task with enthusiasm, declaring the whole tale 'was taken from the American Press of 14 years ago' and that people who talked about UFOs were 'charlatans guilty of self-deception, conceit and conscious falsification who should be punished.'

Fortunately, the radical changes in Russia in recent years

have enabled researchers to draw back the veil on UFOs behind the old 'Iron Curtain'. The evidence which has subsequently come to light suggests that here, too, not only had sightings occurred as regularly as in the West, but the appearance of the objects was much the same, and the pattern of the craft heading in a northerly direction was equally apparent. Here, too, there were all manner of sightings, ranging from those by trained observers such as pilots to ordinary men and women in the street. All were equally convinced about what they had seen—no matter *what* the party line might be.

Sadly, it has proved impossible to discover the fate of Murashov's polar photograph, or any more details about his sighting, but this is offset by another report from the same location in 1956. It was made by the well-known and respected Soviet pilot, Valentin Akkuchatov, who at the time was the chief navigator for the Soviet air base at the North Pole. I quote from a recently translated version made available to UFO researchers through the pages of *New Worlds*:

We were reconnoitring over a strategic ice-area near Greenland when we came out of the clouds into a clear zone and suddenly saw to our left an unknown object flying parallel to us. It seemed like a large, pear-shaped construction, or a lens with pulsating ends. Thinking we had seen an unknown American aircraft, we popped back into the clouds to avoid a meeting. After a further 40 minutes of flying the clouds stopped again and to port we saw the same strange thing once more. It had no wings, antennae or windows, and neither was there any trace of smoke.

We decided to have a close look at the object, so I altered course accordingly. But while we were doing this the object altered its course and remained the same

distance from our machine. After about 15 minutes
the mysterious thing turned down towards the ice and
vanished. It travelled with a speed which to us seemed
impossible.

Akkuchatov's account is interesting for being one of the
earliest in the polar regions to mention a UFO going *down*,
perhaps intent on landing. In later flights, the Soviet pilot
saw other strange objects in the Arctic Circle as well as in
the Baltic regions of Murmansk, Harkov and Gorgi. Here
again his eyewitness accounts of these UFOs all point to a
destination somewhere in the North Pole area.

Two years after Akkuchatov's first sighting, another
intriguing encounter was reported over Kazakhstan on 30
May, 1958, which also contains significant details. The
account was published in the popular magazine, *Smena*,
some three months later.

Between 21.20 and 21.30 Moscow time some people
on a small airfield in the Urals saw a strange object
flying in the north. It shone like a star, but there was
no twinkle. It was visible in the Cassiopeia Constel-
lation but was clearly no higher than 350 metres and
had a velocity of 150 knots. The object veered to the
west and accelerated to 400 knots (the speed of a turbo-
reactor), flying over the airfield without any sound at
all. Then suddenly it stayed motionless in the air for
about 10 seconds. The light now emanating from it
was quite spherical and beams of light could not be
seen. The colour was that of a red rose.

After this, the 'light' started again and went off at
an angle of 45 degrees in a north-westerly direction
for several seconds at 100-120 knots. Thereupon it
suddenly stopped at 45 degrees above the horizon and
the light began to pulsate. Did it then make a spiral

descent? Probably it did. At 80 degrees above the horizon it seemed to turn like a satellite around an (invisible) axis. When the object had become distant it appeared to be approached by a second light coloured like red stars. Both points of light circled each other for a long time and finally disappeared from view heading north.

According to several Western sources, the headquarters of the Russian Space Programme at Sverdlovsk was visited by saucer-shaped UFOs during a 24-hour period in 1959. The objects were picked up by radar arriving from the north 'and caused a certain amount of panic'. In July 1964 a group of people on board a TU 104 flying between Leningrad and Moscow also saw a 'large, bright, metal disc' gliding under their aircraft which disappeared in the direction of the Arctic.

In the Seventies, Siberia was the focal point of a number of UFO reports, especially by people living in the settlement of Polyarny on the coast of the Chukotka Sea in northeast Siberia. They were eyewitnesses to a whole series of phenomena over the North Pole region. Then, in March 1985, it was the turn of an Aeroflot aircrew to go through an experience very similar to that of Captain Terauchi on JAL Flight 1628. The details of this event appeared, curiously, in *Trud*, the trade-union newspaper, and it was the first from Russia to be based on air and ground observation as well as receiving official acknowledgement from the Soviet Academy of Sciences that the crew of Flight 8852 from Tblisi to Tallinn did indeed encounter 'something that we call UFOs'. Things had evidently come a long way since the days of Academician Artsimovich.

The aircraft was flying about 75 miles from Minsk when the co-pilot noticed a 'huge, bright yellow object which emitted a thin ray of light'. Suddenly this widened into a blinding cone, followed by two more cones. The passengers were surprised to see the land below them bathed in bright light and became alarmed as this 'searchlight' settled onto the plane itself. After a few moments, however, the light vanished, leaving a greenish cloud that began to descend at extraordinary speed:

> This 'cloud' eventually took up a position behind the airliner. The pilot alerted ground control which pin-pointed the UFO flying behind the plane at 30,000 feet and at 300 miles an hour. The 'cloud' changed shape into a plum, then a square [see the JAL encounter] and finally 'solidified' as a giant, needle-nosed, wingless aircraft with a curious animal-like tail illuminated by a green and yellow light.

The 'cloud plane' then followed the airliner over Riga and Vilnius, where ground control in both locations picked up two aircraft on their screens when there should only have been one. When the UFO finally swung away from Flight 8852 it was last seen heading north over Tallinn.

Across the Gulf of Riga lies Scandinavia, where Norway and Sweden also have a history of UFO visits. I shall mention just three relevant reports that are representative of a great many more. The first of these took place on 30 June, 1954, when three Scandinavian airliners flew a party of 50 invited scientists and astronomers to watch an eclipse of the sun. Over Telemark, two shiny discs were suddenly spotted travelling towards the northern horizon. A member of the party, Bjorn Bjronulf, said later, 'Amidst all the confusion we realised we were watching something none of us believed in—so-called "flying saucers". But the evidence of our eyes told us differently.' A more down-to-earth experience befell decorator Trygve Jansen in April 1965, while he was returning home from work in Oslo. As he drove along beside the narrow lake of Gjersjoen, he spotted a circle-shaped light flying tremendously fast and high in the sky. 'It was travelling due north and never deviated one way or another. Although I thought it could not possibly be anything made on earth, there was just something about the way that it was travelling that convinced me it must be on the way to *somewhere*. But *where* I have no idea.'

In August 1976, across the border in Sweden, a policeman, Ernst Akerberg, walked into a mystery unlike any he had met before in all his years as a criminal investigator at Visby, on the Baltic island of Gotland. Here, in his own words, is his account as published in *Prediction*:

I had gone with my wife to our fishing cottage at Lergravsviken, about 53 km from Visby. We had just left the cottage for an evening stroll under the full moon when my wife exclaimed, 'Take a look at the sea and see what's coming!' I saw a saucer-like object approaching from a north-easterly direction and heading straight towards us. Its outline was rather blurred and it kept on a straight course until it almost reached the shore. I thought for one moment it might collide with the mountains, but it suddenly tipped up on its edge and went back the way it had come. The last I saw of the UFO was as it disappeared above the north-eastern part of Fitudden Island.

Akerberg's attention to detail would have made him an ideal investigator into the even more mysterious events that occurred in 1952 on the island of Spitsbergen, which lies between Norway and Greenland—events that are still wrapped in a veil of official secrecy. It is a mystery that might well help to resolve the question of whether UFOs do indeed originate from the Hollow Earth, for in that year an unidentified flying object crashed on Spitsbergen after being observed following a flight path that would have taken it directly to the North Pole.

Spitsbergen lies some 700 miles inside the Arctic Circle. It is actually an archipelago of five major islands and its inhabitants are in the curious position of having to look southward to view the Northern Lights. Indeed, were it not for the Gulf Stream, which travels 5,000 miles from Florida to Spitsbergen, there would probably be no shipping to this most northerly community in the world where the sun is never seen from about 26 October to 14 February.

The mystery of Spitsbergan began in the spring of 1952, when several European news agencies reported that a Norwegian air pilot had spotted the wreckage of some kind of aircraft. Apparently, several islanders had seen a 'bright, circular-shaped light' moving directly overhead towards Franz Josef Land, which had suddenly plunged onto a remote part of the main island. Following the pilot's report, rescue teams were flown to the spot, the remains were taken back to Oslo . . . and the controversy began.

Despite repeated requests from the media, it was to be almost three years before an official report on the crash was issued. On 4 September, 1955, Colonel Gernod Darnbyl, the officer who had headed the board of inquiry set up by the Norwegian General Staff, gave an interview to the *Stuttgarter Tageblatt*. For once in the muddied and often controversial history of UFOs, his words did not amount to a cover-up, but were an open and frank statement:

The object which crashed on Spitsbergen was not an aircraft but an object commonly known as a flying saucer. It was seriously damaged and experts from Britain and America were invited to join our investigation. It is still undergoing intensive examination. Although our present knowledge does not yet enable us to solve all the riddles, I am confident that these remains will prove to be of the utmost importance in this respect.

Some time ago a misunderstanding was caused by saying that the disc probably was of Soviet origin. It has—this we wish to state emphatically—not been built in any country on earth. The materials used in its construction are completely unknown to all the experts who participated in the investigation. The board of inquiry is not going to publish an extensive report until some *sensational facts* [my italics] have been discussed with US and British experts.

No further statement on the mystery of the Spitsbergen 'disc' has been issued from that day to this. And all requests to the Norwegian authorities are answered with a polite reply that they have no wish to comment on the affair. As Colonel O. B. Engvik, Air Attaché at the Norwegian Embassy in America, told UFO researcher Robert Loftin recently, 'Our Air Force's UFO material is mainly of a security-graded nature and cannot be put to the disposal of enquiries from the public.' In other words, it is *classified*. My own enquiries to the Norwegian Embassy in London met with a similar response, and a suggestion that I might care to contact one of the UFO groups in Norway which had been investigating the story—bringing me back full circle to the sources that had supplied the information in the first place.

But not quite. A contact in Oslo forwarded to me a copy of a statement made by two Norwegian officers who had served in the Arctic regions after the events on Spitsbergen. Second Lieutenant Brobs and Second Lieutenant Tyllensen both claim to have seen UFOs in the Arctic and maintain that they are sure these craft have landed near the North Pole. In the words of Lieutenant Tyllensen:

I think the Arctic is serving as a kind of base for these unknowns, especially during snow storms when we are being forced back to our bases. Shortly after such adverse weather conditions, I have seen them land and take off on three separate occasions. I noticed then that after having landed they execute a speedy rotation around their discs. A brilliant glow of light, the intensity of which being variable with regard to speed and at landing and take-off, prevents any view of the things happening behind this curtain of light on or inside the disc itself.

Another of my informants, who is familiar with the Arctic region, says that a UFO lies buried near the northernmost tip of Ellesmere Island on the far side of Greenland from Spitsbergen. It, too, allegedly crashed while flying towards the pole. Although no serious attempt has yet been made to excavate the site, the evidence of the object's presence is compelling enough for Dr John M. DeLaurier of the Dominion of Canada Observatory in Ottawa to have instigated a research programme. This he hopes will one day be followed up by a visit to one of the most inhospitable yet fascinating places on earth.

Are both these stories imaginative fantasies or further evidence that the UFOs in our skies may actually originate from a world beneath our feet? Judge for yourself. However, this is not quite the end of our search for answers to the Hollow Earth enigma. There remain two more important questions that demand investigation. The first, which we look at in the next chapter, is, if the inner world is inhabited, *who* might live there?

Eleven

THE INTRATERRESTRIALS

Reinhold Schmidt was a quietly-spoken, rather self-effacing man who lived in an apartment block on Franklin Avenue in what is known as the Hollywood Flats district of Los Angeles. In 1958 he made headline news with a story more startling than any publicist in the film industry could probably have dreamed up. For Schmidt told the press, radio and television that he had been taken in a UFO on a journey to the Arctic and met a group of men and women who lived, he said, *somewhere* beneath the North Pole.

While several of the early champions of the Hollow Earth concept, including Halley, Mather and Symmes, believed the inner world was uninhabited and offered mankind the prospect of a vast new area to colonise, a number of others have claimed that it *is* occupied, and that these subterranean people—the Intraterrestrials—may well have been there for centuries. As O. C. Hugenin wrote in an article, 'The Subterranean World', in the July 1965 issue of *Fate* magazine, 'The idea of the existence of a Subterranean World will shock many people. To others it will sound impossible, for "certainly" they will say, "if it existed, it would have been discovered long ago". But not necessarily so. There may well be good reasons why some antediluvian race which came from the submerged continents of Lemuria or Atlantis and developed a civilisation far beyond ours would wish to keep their existence a secret.'

Reinhold Schmidt's 'contact' is therefore of especial interest because of its comparatively recent date and because it provides further evidence of the origins of UFOs. It was in August 1958 that he first told an LA newspaper about his journey and afterwards repeated the story for the rest of the media and the UFOlogists who came to talk to him. Schmidt never refused an interview and convinced everyone he spoke to of his sincerity. One of them, reporter Charles Longcroft of the *Los Angeles Examiner*, wrote later, 'This was the first time I have ever been face to face with someone who claims to have contacted space men or to have been inside a saucer . . . My impression is that the man has definitely seen something and is not making the whole story up as a publicity stunt.'

The facts about Reinhold Schmidt and his journey to the North Pole are these. He was born in 1920 in Hamburg, from which his parents fled after Hitler's rise to power. The whole family came to California and were granted US citizenship. Reinhold was educated in Los Angeles and followed his father into a small office supply business in the city. He became interested in stories of UFOs, he said, after reading Frank Scully's ground-breaking book *Behind the Flying Saucers* in 1950, but never expected to see one himself. All that changed for him during a few days in August 1958, as he told *UFO Report*:

I had what I thought was a dream telling me to go to a quarry in Bakersfield. In fact I learned later it was a message from the space people. On August 14, I drove my Buick to the quarry and after sitting around for several hours, this circular silver craft came down from the sky. It seemed to be made of something like aluminium and access to it was by sliding doors and a ramp that was lowered to the ground. A figure appeared at the doorway carrying some kind of torch in its hand. This was flashed on me and it paralysed my physical movements for a minute or two without impairing my ability to think or talk.

The figure with the torch was then joined by two others. They came down the ramp and I suddenly found I could move again. They escorted me into the craft. Rather than leave my car in the quarry, one of the people indicated I could take it in the machine and it was driven up the ramp and brought on board. We then took off and flew north towards Alaska and after that up to the Arctic and over the polar regions.

The crew of the craft consisted of four men and two females, Schmidt said. They were all tall, with noble features and dressed in grey, one-piece, skin-tight costumes. The women were especially pretty, in the classical style he always associated with paintings of the ancient Greeks and Romans. They spoke to each other in what he recognised as 'high German' because he had been taught the language by his parents. Throughout the entire journey, however, he was always addressed in very precise English.

What was remarkable about the space craft was that from inside the whole of the hull appeared to be transparent and it was possible to see out from anywhere except those sections which were obscured by machinery or control panels. There were couches, chairs and small tables, and although they did not appear to be fixed to the floor, they never moved even when the craft made the most complex and high speed manoeuvres. I was able to see all the journey up to the Arctic Circle. When we got there we seemed to go under the Arctic Ocean and enter a huge hole. I was conscious of passing over a strange landscape though we never actually landed.

Reinhold Schmidt said that his 'hosts' never told him precisely where they came from, although he became increasingly convinced their homeland must be somewhere in the region of the pole. It was evident from the flying machine that they had a highly mechanised society, and from their manner he guessed they enjoyed comfortable and peaceful lives. If their mission had a purpose, he felt it was to observe mankind and stop us from destroying the planet.

Schmidt's voyage lasted for five days, during which he slept several times. He remembered having the sensation of seeing a land not unlike the earth which was lit by a glowing sun rather different from our Sun. He also twice had the impression of crossing a large curve of ocean when the horizon dipped and fell and then righted itself. On 18 August he was returned to California and once again found himself in the Bakersfield quarry with the Buick beside him. As he stood watching the space craft disappear rapidly northwards, he was suddenly aware that he had an unexpected souvenir of the journey that might help him convince people of the truth of the extraordinary events he had experienced. For he noticed that the paintwork on the upper surfaces of his car had been turned *luminous*.

*   *   *

Several of the very earliest legends of the Hollow Earth claim that it is inhabited by, variously, giants, demonic creatures, 'the little people', and a wise, peaceable humanoid race like that encountered by Reinhold Schmidt. Some researchers believe it may be occupied by the survivors of Lemuria and Atlantis who fled there to escape the deluge which overwhelmed their continents. There is another group who claim the intraterrestrials are the self-same people spoken about with awe in several of the oldest mythologies. They cite the ancient tales of certain humans being guided by godlike creatures—in particular the ancient Greeks and Romans who developed an entire theology based on such beings and believed these 'gods' and 'goddesses' were actually emissaries from the inner world. Historian William F. Warren has commented significantly on this in his book *Paradise Found* (1953): 'Many ancient texts and manuscripts make reference to the "Underworld" as a real and genuine dwelling place. I am of the opinion that religions have failed regarding their teaching of a "Hell" below—because a deep scrutiny of the texts tells more of a "paradise" than a burning abyss.'

The first book to speculate at length on who or what the 'intraterrestrials' might be was by a Scandinavian intellectual at Copenhagen University, Professor Ludvig Holberg (1684–1754). Written in Latin and published in 1741, it was called, *Nicolai Klimii Iter Svbterranevm; Novamtellvris Theoriam as Historiam Qvintae Monarchiae adhvc Nobis Incognitae* (The Journey of Niels Klim to the World Underground). Holberg, who was born in Bergen, Norway, studied in Denmark before becoming a professor at the university, first of philosophy and history, and later of metaphysics and Latin rhetoric. A brilliant and inquisitive scholar, he was inspired to write the book because of a lifelong interest in the curious legends which proliferated in his native Norway about a subterranean world.

Holberg's book tells the story of a man who, while exploring a mountain, accidentally finds his way into the Hollow Earth. Here he discovers a central sun circled by a tiny planet, Nazar, and on the concave shell lives a curious race of intelligent beings. Unlike the world he has just left, however, Niels Klim learns that the females are the dominant sex, and by confining the male population to the most

The Hollow Earth as imagined by Professor Ludvig Holberg of
Copenhagen University.

basic tasks, they have created a utopia of peace and harmony. A map of Holberg's idea of the hollow world is
reproduced here.

It is perhaps not surprising that Holberg chose to write
his work in Latin, because it was swiftly denounced in
Denmark as dangerously radical and was subjected to probably the first attempt to suppress a Hollow Earth theory.
Although an English translation was published the following
year, it was to be almost half a century—and long after the
author's death—before a popular edition in Danish
appeared.

Holberg's book may well have inspired an English
lawyer, Robert Paltock (1698–1767), to ponder on the possibility of a Hollow Earth and who might live there. In any
event, in 1751 Paltock published his own contribution to
the theory, a two-volume work with a title that is so self-

explanatory as to make reading it almost unnecessary: *The Life and Adventures of Peter Wilkins, A Cornish Man: Relating particularly, his Shipwreck near the South Pole; his wonder-ful passage thro' a subterraneous Cavern into a kind of New World; his meeting there with a Gawry or Flying Woman, whose life he preserv'd, and after-wards married her, his extraordinary conveyance to the Country of Glums and Gawrys, or Men and Women that fly. Likewise a Description of this Strange Country, with the Laws, Customs and Manners of its Inhabitants and the Author's Remarkable Transactions among them.*

The title page also refers in similar tone to Wilkins' departure from the inner world in a flying machine (shades of UFOs here), his rescue by a ship, the *Hector*, and his return voyage to Plymouth where, after recounting his story, he died in 1739. The book is embellished with a series of engravings of the Gawries who also rule the roost in a nation where war and the evils of the outer world are unknown. The English poet Samuel Taylor Coleridge called the book 'a work of uncommon beauty' and used some of its ideas in his poem *The Rime of the Ancient Mariner*.

It was probably no intention of either Holberg or Paltock that their readers should believe literally in an inner world full of dominant women or winged people (although they may have liked the idea), but the two books certainly helped to further discussion of the whole legend. One unlikely person to be intrigued by the notion was Giacomo Casanova (1725–98), the Italian libertine, who in 1788 wrote *Icosameron*, a book notable for its realistic tone and excellent scientific speculation—in particular the anticipation of electricity . . . thanks to the help of the intraterrestrials. In this case the subterranean world is occupied by the Megamicres—the 'big-littles'—small people who are large in spirit. They have inhabited their paradise-like world since time immemorial and are said to be without sin. Here again the book was undoubtedly making a point rather than offering a serious proposal.

Less than half a century later, Captain John Cleves Symmes propounded his theory of 'Concentric Spheres' but thought it unlikely that anyone was already living inside the earth. According to Paul Clark in his *Atlantic Monthly* report, Symmes' only significant comment in this respect looked to the future when human beings might be living in *both* dimensions:

> The inhabitants upon the exterior surface, Symmes declared, would be antipodes to those immediately under them, upon the interior surface, as well as to those upon the opposite side of the earth; while the inhabitants of the inner world would be antipodal only to those immediately opposite them upon the outer side, that is to say, the external inhabitants would have two sets of antipodes, while those of the interior would have only one.

Symmes' whole idea did, however, inspire *Symzonia: A Voyage of Discovery* by a certain Captain Adam Seaborn, which was published in 1820 complete with a 'Sectional View of the Earth' showing the openings at both poles.

In the book, Seaborn describes an expedition by sea to find an entrance to the Hollow Earth via the North Pole. The boat is sucked into the interior by a powerful current and there the seafarers discover an enchanted world lit by two suns and a moon. It is inhabited by a race of extremely pale-skinned men and women dressed in white to demonstrate their purity. They appear quiet and gentle, but have developed a fearsome armoury of weapons which they apparently intend to use to keep their world free from contamination by surface *Homo sapiens*. When the crew discover that the inner world is the repository of huge deposits

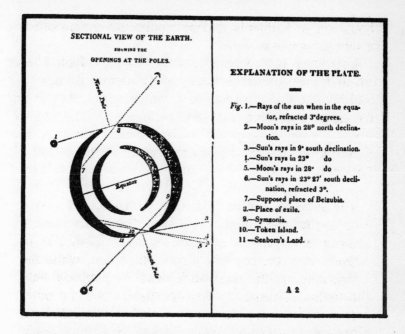

Diagram and explanation of a 'Sectional view of the Earth', which appeared in Captain Adam Seaborn's book *Symzonia*.

of gold and begin casting covetous eyes upon them, they are unceremoniously ordered to leave by the all-powerful ruler of the utopian government.

It has been suggested that Symmes himself might have been 'Captain Adam Seaborn', as the name is so obviously fictitious and nothing whatsoever is known about the writer. However, this is not a view that I and a number of other researchers share because of Symmes' known determination that America should annexe the Hollow Earth, a place he believed to be conducive to mankind and in no way hostile. In an essay, 'The Authorship of *Symzonia*', written for the *New England Quarterly* (June 1975), Hans-Joachim Lang and Benjamin Lease opted for Nathaniel Ames, a writer of stories about the sea; while in a copy of the book held in the Library of Congress in Washington, the authorship is credited to one Jared Sparks.

Some thirty years after *Symzonia* was published, however, two bona-fide seamen were credited with having led expeditions to find entrances to Symmes' world. A note in *Isis* magazine of December 1941 records:

Captain Wiggins, an Englishman, read a paper to the 'Society of Arts' in John Street, Adelphi, about his voyage to a subterranean world. The explorer, after passing the 80 degree line, saw a timbered country with an abundance of animal life and whose inhabitants spoke Hebrew and possessed a superior culture. Perhaps these were the descendants of the lost tribes of Israel, the Captain said, who went up the Euphrates to the north to dwell in a land where man had never dwelt before. Around this same time, Captain Tuttle, an old United States whaling master, visited 'Symzonia': his account being similar to the preceding one, save that he states that every fourth winter is mild and that the land can be reached only by steam vessel.

Willis George Emerson, who related Olaf Jansen's visit to the inner world in 1908, said the old man told him just before he died that the place was inhabited by a race of fair-skinned giants. The men were all twelve feet tall and the women a couple of feet shorter. Both sexes wore embroidered tunics and sandals on their feet. They were mild-tempered, dignified and lived for over five hundred years. According to Jansen they also possessed a mysterious power, much greater than electricity, which they used to drive their machinery and equipment. (This sounds to me rather like the 'Vril-power' which I discussed at length in my earlier book, *The Lost World of Agharti*, published in 1982.)

The Brazilian naval commander Paulo Strauss (see Chapter Nine) takes a similar view, and has his own theory about one of the great disappearance stories of this century:

> The subterranean people have a physical structure that resembles those on the surface, but they are much more advanced than us. Among their number are certain people who descended from the surface and decided to stay, including Colonel Percy Fawcett, the English explorer who disappeared in 1925 while exploring with his son, Jack. They were not killed by Indians in the Matto Grosso as is commonly supposed, but found an entrance to the Hollow World, descended, and there remained. For years afterwards, Fawcett's wife claimed to be in telepathic touch with her husband in a subterranean world.

Raymond Palmer, whose acquaintance we made in Chapter Eight, in 1945 published a series of narratives in *Amazing Stories*, said to be based on 'racial memory', which maintained there was not one, but two, races living in the Hollow Earth. In these accounts, 'written' by Richard S. Shaver (1907–75), a Pennsylvania psychic, which commenced with 'I Remember Lemuria' in March 1945, it was stated that the interior of the earth was inhabited by the remnants of a migration of surface-dwellers who had been forced to seek shelter underground more than 12,000 years earlier, and there had become divided into two groups. One of these, the 'abandoneros' (shortened to 'deros') were technically very advanced but evil-intentioned. They had flying machines (UFOs again) and a variety of sinister machines that could be used to create an 'urge to kill' in unsuspecting victims. It was these deros, Shaver claimed, who were responsible for much of the evil in the world—wars, accidents, murders and suicides. Their worst depredations were, however, sometimes thwarted by a dwindling number of highly intelligent and pacifist members of the original race known as the 'teros'.

Not surprisingly, there has been a great deal of debate about these stories—often referred to as 'The Shaver Mystery'—and described by *Life* magazine as 'the most celebrated rumpus to rock the science fiction world'. But all through his life, Richard Shaver said he believed implicitly in what he had written. 'I am no scientist,' he insisted in one defence of the series, 'but I have studied all the scientific books I can get—only to become more and more convinced that I have remembered *true* things.'

Perhaps even more curious still is the eyewitness account by an American geologist who was among a group of scientists working in Antarctica in 1958 during International Geophysical Year. The man was conducting experiments with a colleague on the Knox coast when their visibility was suddenly obscured by a 'violent whirl of white' which he knew could not be a meteorological effect. Certain there was no one else in the vicinity, the two men walked towards the whirlwind and discovered that it was caused not by snow but by a kind of hot, white steam with a sharp smell which they could not define. In the middle of the cloud, as it dissolved, they saw a dome-shaped structure about two metres high with a diameter of about ten metres. It was shining like glass.

Although I am satisfied as to the qualifications and honesty of the two scientists in this story, I have been asked not to name them. But here in his own words is the statement of one of the pair.

The first thing I thought of was of something unknown below the ground, perhaps of volcanic origin. Being both fascinated and frightened at the same time, I ran towards the dome. At first I thought someone had got there before me when I saw two moving figures; but immediately afterwards my blood froze as they were not human at all but round 'things', yellowish and with a height of hardly more than a metre, like balloons but clumsy on the ice and only half inflated, tottering and wheeling around.

Near them or on them there was a light which seemed to me like an oxyacetylene lamp. A little ball seemed to explode in front of me, spreading a crackling shower of blue sparks. I started to run as I was in a real panic. 'Get away!' I shouted to my friend who had stayed behind, 'Get away, quick!' We only turned round to look when we were back in the safety of our transport. For a few moments we saw the reflections of the dome and then another white whirl. There was a reflection in the sky but scarcely visible, and when the cloud faded there was nothing at all on the ice.

Opinions are divided about precisely what the two men saw. The account suggests they may have come across a UFO which had landed on the ice, perhaps prior to entering the southern entranceway to the Hollow Earth. But if that is so, the identity of the 'things' in the machine seems to suggest extraterrestrials as more likely inhabitants than humanoids.

One more report brings our history up to date. According to an article in *The National Enquirer* of 25 February, 1992, a Danish scientist and explorer, Edmund Bork, had recently returned from leading an international team of explorers through the North Pole opening the previous summer. He had apparently found the 1,400 mile-wide opening thanks to studying the ESSA-7 satellite photograph. The Dane told one of the newspaper's reporters:

There's a hole in the pole and it leads to a tropical paradise located at the centre of the earth. It has its own sun, a shallow, warm water sea, and lush, tropical vegetation. What's more the land within is inhabited by a highly advanced and very peaceful race of humans. Normally the hole cannot be seen from the air because of the heavy cloud cover over the North Pole and because the inhabitants of the Hollow Earth keep it covered with electronic 'light screens'. These screens give the illusion of vast fields of ice and snow through holographic manipulation of the snow and ice surrounding the hole. Because the hole is so large, the slope down is very gradual and any explorers are hardly aware they are entering another world.

The National Enquirer added by way of a footnote: 'A number of other men claim to have entered the hole at the North Pole. They include William Shavers, a Navy pilot who crashed at the North Pole during World War Two. A tribe of wandering Eskimos also told a Canadian reporter in 1956 that they had found 'a green land at the top of the world.'

This last sentence deserves more than just a passing reference because a number of explorers and researchers believe the Inuit are intimately connected with the Hollow Earth legend, and may even have originated there. Certainly, they remain one of the most mysterious people on earth, living in the world's most hostile environment, and about whose origins no one can be really sure. Some authorities believe they are the oldest inhabitants of the northern hemisphere, existing in a region for which nature never intended human beings and into which they came by chance.

The Norwegian explorer Nansen, in his book *In Northern Mists* (1911), writes at some length about his experiences with the Eskimos or Inuit and declares at one point:

When we remember that in the efforts of the Eskimos to tell us where they came from, they would point to the north and describe a land of perpetual sunshine, it is easy to see that the Norwegians who associate the polar regions with the end of the world, certainly not with a new world, would wonder at the strange origin thus indicated. No wonder we regard them as a super-natural people who may well have come from the interior of the Earth.

In 1909, while Rear Admiral Robert Peary was exploring at the North Pole, he was surprised to learn that his Eskimo guides believed he was 'on an expedition to find the "great people" to the north, from which they were descended.' Peary understood them to mean a paradise where the inhabitants possessed great powers. From what he was able to deduce of their religion, his Eskimos believed that after death they would 'descend beneath the earth where the sun never sets and the waters never freeze'.

Charles Berlitz, in his *World of Strange Phenomena*, tells the story of two archaeologists, Magnus Marks and Froelich Rainey, who carried out excavations at Ipiutak in June 1940. There they discovered the ancient ruins of what they could only describe as an 'Arctic Metropolis'. Rows of buried stones and elaborate Eskimo carvings pointed to the fact that there had once been as many as 800 habitations extending along the shore for almost a mile, home to around 4,000 people. According to Rainey this amounted to an incredible number of inhabitants for a hunting village in the Arctic, and he theorised, 'The people of this Arctic Metropolis brought their arts from some centre of cultural advance.'

In his book *Not of this World*, Peter Kolosimo points out with equal significance: 'The Eskimos believe they were deported from regions which today are tropical by the use of "huge metal birds" [UFOs yet again!]. Another legend among them just as current is that some of their forefathers, now dead or "carried off into the skies", returned afterwards with magical powers they never had before.'

William Reed and Marshall B. Gardner, both of whom drew heavily on the accounts of Nansen and Peary in their books, came to much the same conclusion about the origins of the Eskimos, as Theodore Fitch has noted in *Our Paradise Inside the Earth*: 'Both Reed and Gardner declared that there must be a land of paradise on the other side of the mammoth ice barrier. Both men were of the opinion that a race of little brown people lived in the interior of the Earth. It is possible that the Eskimos descended from these people.'

Indeed it is. As recently as 26 April, 1998, the London newspaper *The Sunday Times* reported: 'A lost tribe of dark-skinned Eskimos has been discovered living on the edge of the icefields at the North Pole.' Scientists, it said, were hoping to be able to study the men and women, their lifestyle, culture and traditions, as well as any differences between them and their paler brethren. Only time will tell if this enquiry might prove a major step along the way to solving another of the mysteries of the Hollow Earth enigma: who, if anyone, lives there.

Twelve

A UNIVERSE OF HOLLOW WORLDS?

During a research visit to the headquarters of the National Aeronautics and Space Administration (NASA) in Washington DC, I had the opportunity to look at some of the remarkable photographs that have been taken by American spacecraft of the planets and moons in our solar system. These breath-taking colour pictures, filmed in close-up by the various passing probes, reveal the Moon, Mars, Venus, Jupiter, Saturn and the other heavenly bodies not just as specks in the enormity of space but as truly amazing worlds. The details are so clear that a viewer feels on the verge of touch-down on places that have haunted our imagination for centuries.

It was while I was looking at a particularly vivid photograph of Callisto, one of the moons of Jupiter, that a startling thought occurred to me. The picture had been taken by Voyager 2 in July 1979 and showed the surface of the little moon—one of four major satellites and twelve smaller moons that orbit the most massive of all the planets in our system—sparkling with lights which appeared to be shining through holes in its surface. It seemed to all intents and purposes like a giant globe illuminated from the *inside*. The idea was electrifying. Could it, too, be a hollow world? I wondered, studying the moon even closer. And if this was true of Callisto, could there be others—thereby making the Earth just one of many such in the galaxy?

I have since discovered that others have had similar thoughts and have come to the conclusion that we might well be living in a whole universe of hollow worlds. What might be true in the formation of one planet could surely be possible for others, too.

Looking for facts to substantiate this theory took me back once again to Symmes who, of course, used the planet Saturn as part of his argument. Sure enough, Paul Clark, the note-taker at the captain's lecture, had not missed the relevant statement, although he was unfortunately brief on the matter. I quote from his *Atlantic Monthly* resumé: 'Captain Symmes maintained that the other planets, like the earth, were each composed of concentric spheres; but I have not space sufficient to refer to the telescopic appearances which are noticed by him in support of his theory.'

Evidence suggests that Symmes' son, Americus, picked up on this point, too, for according to an essay, 'The Theory of Concentric Spheres' by William Marion Miller in *Isis* (December 1941), 'The Younger Symmes later marshalled and elaborated essentially the same facts in support of the theory—the rings of Saturn, as proof of the theory of concentricity in nature, as are the horns of Venus and the belt of Jupiter.'

When Marshall B. Gardner came to write his book *A Journey to the Earth's Interior* in the early years of this century, he went rather deeper to substantiate the idea.

When we say that the Earth is a hollow body with polar openings and an interior sun, we back up the statement by referring to nebulas in many stages of evolution in which the gradual forming of the outer envelope of the future planet and the interior sun, and even the beginnings of the polar openings, are all clearly visible in their different stages. Then we point to the actual construction of the planets, Mars, Venus and Mercury, and we show just what the polar openings are like. We show that they are not just ice caps, because direct light has been seen to come from them. And then we demonstrate conclusively that the Earth, like Mars and the other planets, has its polar openings, too.

Curiously, it was to be another fifty years before any Hollow Earth researcher looked heavenwards to support the concept. And when one did, the result was a court case and humiliation for the proposer of a *hollow sun*. Martin Gardner gives the facts in his excellent work *Fads and Fallacies in the Name of Science* (1957):

In 1952 a West German patent attorney, Godfried Bueren, offered 25,000 marks to anyone who could disprove his Hollow Sun theory. According to Bueren, the sun's flaming outer shell surrounds a cool inner sphere. Covered with vegetation, the dark core can be glimpsed occasionally through sunspots which are nothing more than temporary rents in the blazing shell. The German Astronomical Society carefully ripped the theory apart and when Bueren refused to pay, the society took legal action. Incredible as it may seem, the court decided in favour of the astronomers. Bueren was ordered to pay the sum he had offered, plus court costs and interest.

The German's concept is certainly a difficult one to image. Much more likely is the idea that the Moon could be hollow, as was first proposed in January 1970 by two Russian scientists, Mikhail and Alexandra Chtcherbakov of the Soviet Academy of Sciences. In an article published in *Komsolol-*

skaya Pravda, the couple rejected the three general hypotheses about the Moon's origin: (1) that it was a piece of the Earth that had been torn away; (2) that it had been formed independently from the same cloud of gas and dust; and (3) that it had wandered into the solar system from far away and been caught by the Earth's gravity.

The Chtcherbakovs said that the Moon's low density compared to that of the Earth suggested to them that it was actually a hollow sphere:

> This appears to consist of two shells containing an atmosphere, the inner 30 kms thick made of extremely hard metal, the outer about 4 kms thick composed of thermo-protective, resistant and inoxydizable rocks including chromium, titanium and zirconium. The larger lunar craters and their surprisingly small depths were caused by meteorites striking the metallic 'shock absorbers' and exploding sideways not inwards, causing extensive shallow holes and scattering debris far and wide.'

What made the two Russians' theory really fascinating was their contention that the Moon is actually an *artificial* satellite that was once launched on a geocentric orbit around the Earth by alien beings of enormous intelligence whose civilisation was based on a giant spaceship:

> Inside the hollow interior of the Moon are storerooms for propulsives, tools and materials for repairs, navigational equipment and observational instruments. Some lunar rocks are different and older than terrestrial rocks. This does not prove the Moon was fabricated before Earth was formed, but it is undoubtedly extremely ancient. The satellite, now probably uninhabited, is becoming a wreck, the stabilizers no longer function,

the poles are displaced, and the face opposite Earth
wobbles badly. The dark 'maria' or 'dried seas' seem
to be patches of the metallic inner sphere stripped of
its protective sheath, later repaired. The repair material
and equipment underneath these localities explain the
phenomena of 'mascons', zones of increased gravity
discovered in eccentric orbits of our own lunar satellites. Gas sometimes seen escaping through craters is
not due to volcanic activity but to leakage of atmosphere inside from fissures in the outer sphere.

Startling as this idea must have seemed at first to many
readers, it soon attracted serious attention in America,
especially from the science writer Don Wilson, who published a series of essays in *Fate* magazine giving various
examples of how strange a place the Moon quite evidently
was. He cited a number of curious phenomena that had been
observed and measured on the surface by astronomers all
over the world, including clouds of water vapour and mysterious winking lights. He drew attention to the fact that
the average density of the Moon was the same as lightweight
aluminium, and printed a new photograph of a crater at the
Moon's South Pole which was very much deeper than any
of the others. He suggested that this just might be an
entranceway to the hollow interior, very similar to those in
the Arctic and Antarctic regions on Earth, and went on:

The seismic data from the Moon is also extremely
impressive. Scientists were literally falling off their
chairs when it first started to come in. The analysis
done by the scientists at NASA in 1962 seemed to point
to only one conclusion—the Moon must be hollow!

In astronomy, mass is dealt with on the basis of
relative masses. This being so, if the Moon is hollow,
then so might be the Earth and other planets and their

satellites because gravity is based on masses—relative masses and distances. Therefore if only *one* object was hollow it would be patently different from all the rest.

Subsequent study by a number of Hollow Earth researchers has produced a list of those planets and moons *most likely* to be hollow, and I propose to look at the evidence for them one at a time. They are, after the Earth and the Moon: Mercury, Venus, Mars and its moon Phobos, Jupiter and its satellite Callisto, Saturn and, just possibly, the two very recently discovered moons of Uranus.

MERCURY is, of course, the planet nearest the Sun and is believed to have the harshest environment of any world in the solar system. Its appearance is not unlike that of the Moon, with many well-defined craters and, significantly, an interior said to 'very strongly resemble our own', according to a NASA scientist after the flypast of Mariner 10 in 1974. Mercury has a curiously weak magnetic field which gives it an unusual axis of spin and this is what first led to suggestions that it might be hollow.

Astronomers in the past have several times noticed a tiny, bright dot on the planet during a Mercurial eclipse. This caused Raymond Palmer to speculate, in an article in *The Hidden World*, 'if it isn't true that just at that moment, the polar orifice of Mercury, formed as other bodies by a vortexial action, presents itself at precisely the proper position to be observed?' Further discussion has followed a report in the April 1992 issue of *Final Frontier* on this same phenomenon. 'Despite temperatures that can climb as high as 800 degrees Fahrenheit,' the journal stated, 'researchers at the California Institute of Technology in Pasadena have identified what they believe is a water ice-cap more than 180 miles in diameter on Mercury's north pole.'

VENUS is often referred to as 'Earth's Sister Planet', being our closest neighbour at a distance of just 26,000,000 miles. Space probes from both Russia and the USA have penetrated the blankets of yellowish clouds which cover the planet. These proved to be almost 95 per cent carbon dioxide—with a hint of sulphur dioxide providing the colour—while traces of water vapour were also recorded. The surface of Venus is covered by vast rolling plains and four major highland regions dotted with a number of active volcanoes.

The annals of astronomy tell us that twice, in 1686 and 1833, 'bright lights' were observed shining out of Venus' North and South Poles. Then, in 1978, a Pioneer 12 orbiting vehicle revealed 'holes' in the atmosphere just above the North and South Poles. A decade later even more significant evidence was revealed when NASA's Jet Propulsion Laboratory released a series of radar-generated photographs of the planet which pierced through the clouds, one of the images clearly showing a *north polar opening*. The picture had such an impact on the scientific community that it was published on the front cover of the April 1989 issue of *Discovery* magazine.

MARS, the 'Red Planet', has probably excited more interest than any of the other worlds in the solar system—and, certainly, the most widespread speculation that it could contain life. The stories about its so-called 'canals' are part of scientific folklore, and books such as H. G. Wells' *The War of the Worlds* (1898) have given it a unique place in speculative fiction. With its erratic motion, white-capped poles and dark, blue-grey formations in a constant state of change, the chances of it being hollow are considered to be very high. Mars has a day almost identical to ours, although its atmosphere is much thinner and consists mostly of carbon dioxide. The temperatures are such as to prevent water existing for long as a liquid, changing directly from vapour to ice and back again.

The US astronomer Percival Lowell (1855–1916), who first suggested there might be life on Mars as a result of observing the criss-crossing pattern of lines he identified as 'canals', was also the first to theorise that the planet might be hollow. He spotted through his telescope 'a dark, circular band' appearing around the poles during one summer season, and the following spring noticed something even stranger. 'As I was watching the planet, I saw suddenly two points like stars flash out in the midst of the north polar cap. Dazzlingly white upon the duller white background of the snow, these stars shone brightly for a few moments and then slowly disappeared.' Could these have been rays of light from a central sun inside Mars? A contemporary science writer, Martin Caidin, has also reported that in recent years several American and Russian astronomers have observed very bright flashes originating from both the North and South Poles of Mars. Ernest L. Norman, an American scientific researcher of the paranormal, claims in his book *The Truth About Mars* (1998) that not only is the planet hollow, but that it is actually inhabited by a highly intelligent humanoid race. He writes:

> On Mars the cities are all underground, and as the outside temperature is very rare and of a low oxygen content, they are becoming less and less dependent on that source of air supply. Many thousands of years ago the Martians learned how to obtain air from water by electrolysis ... They are a quiet, peace-loving people who originally migrated there in a space craft from a dying planet and settled below the hostile surface ...

PHOBOS is the closer to the planet of Mars' two moons— about 5,830 miles away—and a strong case has been made that it, too, is hollow inside. The little satellite, about twenty miles in diameter, has a unique orbit of just over seven hours, which means that it travels round the planet *twice* in a Martian day. The moon's surface contains numerous grooves up to 220 yards wide and several craters, the largest of which has been named Stickney. All are believed to have resulted from the impact of missiles from space. Photographs of Phobos taken by the Viking spacecraft in the late Seventies give it the eerie appearance of an alien craft in perpetual orbit around Mars.

JUPITER is the largest planet in the solar system—1,300 Earths would fit comfortably into its bulk—and the first of the four planets, beyond the asteroid belt, which make up the Jovian group with Saturn, Uranus and Neptune. It is famous for its 'Great Red Spot', a strange phenomenon big enough to hold two Earths, and is a mysterious world that has fascinated astronomers for generations. There was general amazement, however, in 1979 when Voyager 1 flew past Jupiter, revealing that the spot is actually a vortex piercing the planet's three distinct zones of water, ammonium hydrosulphide and ammonia, right down to the surface! This has prompted speculation that Jupiter could be in fact hollow, with at least one entranceway far more visible than those on Earth or any of the other planets. Voyager 1 also confirmed that Jupiter was probably originally formed from a swirling mass of dust and gas and can actually be compared to a gigantic 'bag' of gases, consisting of hydrogen and helium in vast 'shells' thousands of miles thick. Just *what* lies at their heart is the real puzzle of Jupiter.

CALLISTO, the moon of Jupiter which first excited my interest in the possibility of other hollow worlds, is said by NASA scientists to be perhaps the only spot in the Jovian system upon which mankind might feasibly land at some time in the future. The farthest of Jupiter's four major Galilean satellites, named after Galileo who discovered them in 1610 (the other three are Io, Europa and Ganymede), Callisto is about 3,000 miles in diameter and is believed to be covered by a soft ice mantle and a thick ice crust. It has probably more craters on its surface than any other moon or planet in the solar system, the result of being regularly bombarded by meteors throughout its entire existence. The most curious sight of all is a 378 mile-wide crater at the heart of a series of concentric rings extending for at least 620 miles in all directions. Could this be an opening to the interior?

SATURN is one of the wonders of the solar system with its unmistakable ring. It hangs in the heavens like a huge, glowing ball with its cluster of satellites, orbiting leisurely around the sun once every 29 years. For a long time Saturn was mistakenly believed to be three planets, and it was not until 1659 that a Dutch astronomer, Christiaan Huygens, defined it as a single world 'surrounded by a thin, flat ring, which nowhere touches the body'. It was Voyager 1 which provided the first close-up views of this romantic world, revealing that the ring-system actually consists of 300 'ringlets' of solid particles of rock and ice. These do not gradually merge into one another as conventional theory would have it, but are separated by complicated gravitational interactions between the ring material and six of Saturn's 15 moons. Whether the rings were created at the same time as the planet, or are the remnants of a comet or moon that passed too close and was torn apart and swirled into orbit, remains a mystery. Saturn takes about ten Earth hours to revolve, and is flatter at the poles than most other planets in the solar system. The complexity of the ring has generated much speculation about the true nature of the planet, not forgetting the white oval spots on the surface which the NASA spacecraft also photographed. The bands of lighter and darker clouds, indicating equatorial and temperate belts, are equally puzzling, although once again, the fact that the planet consists of ice, hydrogen and helium with a certain amount of liquefied rock has fuelled speculation that it, too, may be hollow.

URANUS, the blue-green disc on the far frontier of the solar system, is the third largest body in the system. With a diameter four times that of Earth, it is not unlike Jupiter and Saturn and possesses a dense hydrogen atmosphere. Uranus has an extraordinary orbit, with an axial tilt of 98 degrees relative to the plane of its orbit—which means that first one pole and then the other points directly at the Sun during the course of its 84-year orbit. Both of these poles are noticeably flattened. In complete contrast, the planet rotates very quickly on its axis, turning once every 15 hours. Naturally, this results in the most bizarre 'seasons' on Uranus, with long, intense periods of light and dark. A number of dark spots have been sighted on the surface along with two rather dusky-looking poles, and these have prompted speculation that there may well be disturbances taking place *inside* the planet.

Two small newly identified moons, both far distant from Uranus and as yet unnamed, have added to the planet's mystery. They were discovered in April 1998 by a team of astronomers led by Dr Brett Gladman of the University of Toronto, using cameras mounted on the 16-foot Hale Telescope at Palomar Observatory. The pair have been added to the planet's known five—Oberon, Titania, Ariel, Umbriel and Miranda—and are said to be 40 and 80 miles in diameter respectively and unusually red in colour. Initial observation of the moons by Dr Gladman suggests they may have originated in the outer solar system and been 'captured' by the gravitational pull of Uranus. Again, the similarity between these two curious bodies and Phobos and Callisto has led to speculation that they might also be hollow.

It now seems evident to me that the farther we go into the depths of space, the stronger the possibility becomes that the Earth may be just one of many hollow worlds. Admittedly this is a theory that the majority of scientists and astronomers regard with a good deal of scepticism. None of them, however, have managed to produce enough facts *totally* to disprove such an idea.

There is one further concept that intrigues me as much as it does others who have studied the Hollow Earth enigma. It is this. The search for intelligent life in the galaxy—in particular NASA's SETI programme—has so far drawn a blank despite a great deal of scientific experimentation which included the dispatching of a number of probes into deepest space. Yet even so, we remain convinced that we are not, *cannot* be, alone. So is the simple truth that we are looking in the wrong place?

Is it possible that the Earth is the only planet on which life exists on the *outside*? Could it be that elsewhere in the galaxy life-forms have chosen to dwell *inside* their worlds, protected from harsh environments or the danger from space represented by meteors or comets that could destroy entire populations on impact? Even though we inhabit a world which enables life to flourish on the surface, can we really be certain this is the norm?

The primary requirement for life anywhere is generally agreed to be a sun, and if one was created in the interior when a planet itself was being born, the situation would be half resolved. If this sun were in proportion to the subterranean world it had to light and heat, and did not have to send its rays across the enormity of space like our Sun, the equation would surely be complete. As I have shown in the pages of this book, the concept of a 'paradise' somewhere inside the Earth has been an integral part of myth, folklore and religion since time immemorial—and the significance of this is not beyond a rational explanation. One of the greatest challenges open to mankind must be the final resolution of this enigma: Is a whole new world awaiting us as it has done for ages, not in the far reaches of space but beneath our very feet?

EPILOGUE

In June 1998, a worldwide group of scientists announced the setting up of a co-operative project, Deep Earth Observations from the Sea Floor (DEOS), to 'probe deep under the surface of the earth to search for new lifeforms and answers to some of the planet's most enduring geological mysteries.'

The project will employ a global satellite network working in conjunction with a series of sea-floor observatories and detectors to look beneath the earth's crust for the first time. With the aid of sound and electromagnetic waves that can travel through the planet, the team hopes to find evidence to show precisely what lies deep inside the planet. A leading member, John Orcutt, Professor of Geophysics at the University of California, said it was hoped the project would do for geologists what the Hubble space telescope was doing for astronomers—provide an unprecedented view into undiscovered regions. 'We have long needed a system like Hubble,' Orcutt said, 'but to look inwards not out. This network will be critical for earth sciences and will lead to new insights.'

Another senior scientist, Professor Bob Detrick of the Woods Hole Oceanographic Institution in Massachusetts, added even more significantly, 'The project will allow us to image the interior of the Earth with much greater precision and clarity so we can see how it affects the movements of the continents, the origins of volcanoes and, on a more local scale, the processes that generate earthquakes.'

At an even greater depth, it is hoped that DEOS will give an accurate picture of the world's core. 'It is something that people have been wondering about for centuries,' said Jeremy Bloxham, Professor of Geophysics at Harvard University and another key member of the team. 'I certainly think these sea-floor observatories will help us to crack this complex problem.'

Is the two thousand-year-old South American prophecy about to be fulfilled?

BIBLIOGRAPHY

Berlitz, Charles. *World of Strange Phenomena*, Wynwood Press, 1990.

Bernard, Dr Raymond. *The Hollow Earth*, Health Research, 1960.

Brennan, J. H. *Occult Reich*, Futura Publications, 1974.

Byrd, Richard E. *Little America*, Putnam, 1931.

Charroux, Robert. *The Mysterious Unknown*, Neville Spearman, 1972.

Charroux, Robert. *Lost Worlds*, Souvenir Press, 1973.

Drake, W. Raymond. *Gods and Spacemen in the Ancient West*, Sphere Books, 1974.

Drake, W. Raymond. *Gods and Spacemen in Greece and Rome*, Sphere Books, 1976.

Fitch, Theodore. *Our Paradise Inside the Earth*, published by the author, 1987.

Gardner, Marshall B. *A Journey to the Earth's Interior*, Aurora, 1913.

Gardner, Martin. *Fads and Fallacies in the Name of Science*, Dover, 1957.

Giannini, F. A. *World Beyond the Poles*, Health Research, 1959.

King, Francis, *Satan and the Swastika*, Mayflower Books, 1976.

Kolosimo, Peter. *Not of this World*, Souvenir Press, 1970.

Michell, John and Rickard, Robert J. M. *Phenomena*, Thames & Hudson, 1977.

Nansen, Fridtjof. *In Northern Mists*, Constable & Co., 1911.

Norman, Ernest L. *The Truth About Mars*, Unarius, 1998.

Norman, Eric. *This Hollow Earth*, Lancer Books, 1972.

Norman, Eric. *Gods, Demons and Space Chariots*, Lancer Books, 1970.

Pauwels, Louis and Bergier, Jacques. *The Morning of the Magicians*, Gibbs & Phillips, 1963.

Pennick, Nigel. *Hitler's Secret Sciences*, Neville Spearman, 1981.

Reed, William. *The Phantom of the Poles*, Walter S. Rockey Co., 1906.

Sanderson, Ivan T. *Invisible Residents*, World Publishing Co., 1970.

Sayce, A. M. *Records of the Past*, Doubleday, 1923.

Steiger, Brad. *Worlds Before Our Own*, Star Books, 1980.

Tarde, Gabriel. *Underground Man*, Duckworth & Co., 1905.

Trench, Brinsley Le Poer. *Operation Earth*, Neville Spearman, 1969.

Trench, Brinsley Le Poer. *The Eternal Subject*, Souvenir Press, 1973.

Trench, Brinsley Le Poer. *Secret of the Ages*, Souvenir Press, 1974.

Vallee, Jacques, *Anatomy of a Phenomenon*, Neville Spearman, 1966.

Warren, William F. *Paradise Found*, New Worlds, 1953.

Wilkins, Harold T. *Flying Saucers on the Moon*, Peter Owen, 1954.

Wright, S. Fowler. *The World Below*, Books for Today, 1929.

ACKNOWLEDGEMENTS

These writers whose works I consulted are acknowledged in the text, but I should like to record especial thanks to the following for comments and advice: Robert Anderson, Charles Berlitz, Dr Raymond Bernard, Peter Berresford Ellis, Mark Harp, Paul Jensen, Elizabeth Jordan, Jan Lamprecht, Cate Malone, Albert McDonald, Eric Norman, Robert J. M. Rickard, Paulo Strauss and Professor Thomas Westropp. Members of the staff at the Library of Congress, Washington, the New York Public Library, the British Museum and the British Newspaper Library in London also assisted me in many equally important ways.

I am grateful to the National Aeronautics and Space Administration (NASA) in Washington, the Harvard Library, Boston, and Adventures Unlimited Press of Kempton, Illinois, for the photographs used in the book; the remainder are from my own archives. The following publishers, newspapers and magazines have also allowed me to quote from their publications: Wynwood Press for *World of Strange Phenomena* by Charles Berlitz; Thames & Hudson for *Phenomena* by John Michell and Robert J. M. Rickard; Souvenir Press for *Dimensions* by Jacques Vallee and *Not of this World* by Peter Kolosimo; Putnam for *Records of the Past* by A. M. Sayce and the extracts from *Little America* and *Skyward* by Rear Admiral Richard Byrd; the Hollow Earth Society of Australia and the Library of Congress, Washington, for Byrd's 'Diary'; Avon Books for *The Morning of the Magicians* by Louis Pauwels and Jacques Bergier; Neville Spearman and C. W. Daniel Co. for *Hitler's Secret Sciences* by Nigel Pennick and *The Mysterious Unkown* by Robert Charroux; Walker Publishing Co for *Lost Worlds* by Robert Charroux; Health Research for *Worlds Beyond the Poles* by F. A. Giannini and *The Hollow Earth* by Dr. Raymond Bernard; Peter Owen Ltd for *Flying Saucers on the Moon* by Harold T. Wilkins; New Worlds Publishing for *Paradise Found* by William F. Warren and quotes by Albert McDonald; Vantage Press for *Our Paradise Inside the Earth* by Theodore Fitch; Dover Books for *Fads and Fallacies in the Name of Science* by Martin Gardner; Unarius Academy of Science for *The Truth About Mars* by Ernest L. Norman; Ziff-Davis Publications for the extracts by Raymond Palmer from *Amazing Stories* and *The Hidden World*; *Flying Saucer Review* and the Estate of the Earl of Clancarty (Brinsley Le Poer Trench); *UFO Report* and Gambi Publications for the Reinhold Schmidt statement; *The Sunday Times*; *Atlantic Monthly*; *O Estado de Sao Paulo* and *O Cruziero* of Brazil; *Christchurch Press*, New Zealand; *Royal Irish Academy Journal*; *Journal of the Royal Astronomical Society of Canada*; *New York Daily News*; *Smena*; *Trud*; *Stuttgarter Tageblatt*; *Isis*; *The National Enquirer*; *Komsoloskaya Pravda*; *Nexus*, *Exposure*; *Aurora*; *Prediction*; *Popular Astronomy*; *The Unknown*; *Fate* and *The Final Frontier*. Extracts from the Authorized version of The Bible (The King James Bible), the rights in which are vested in the Crown, are reproduced by permission of the Crown's Patentee, Cambridge University Press.

AM, March 1999